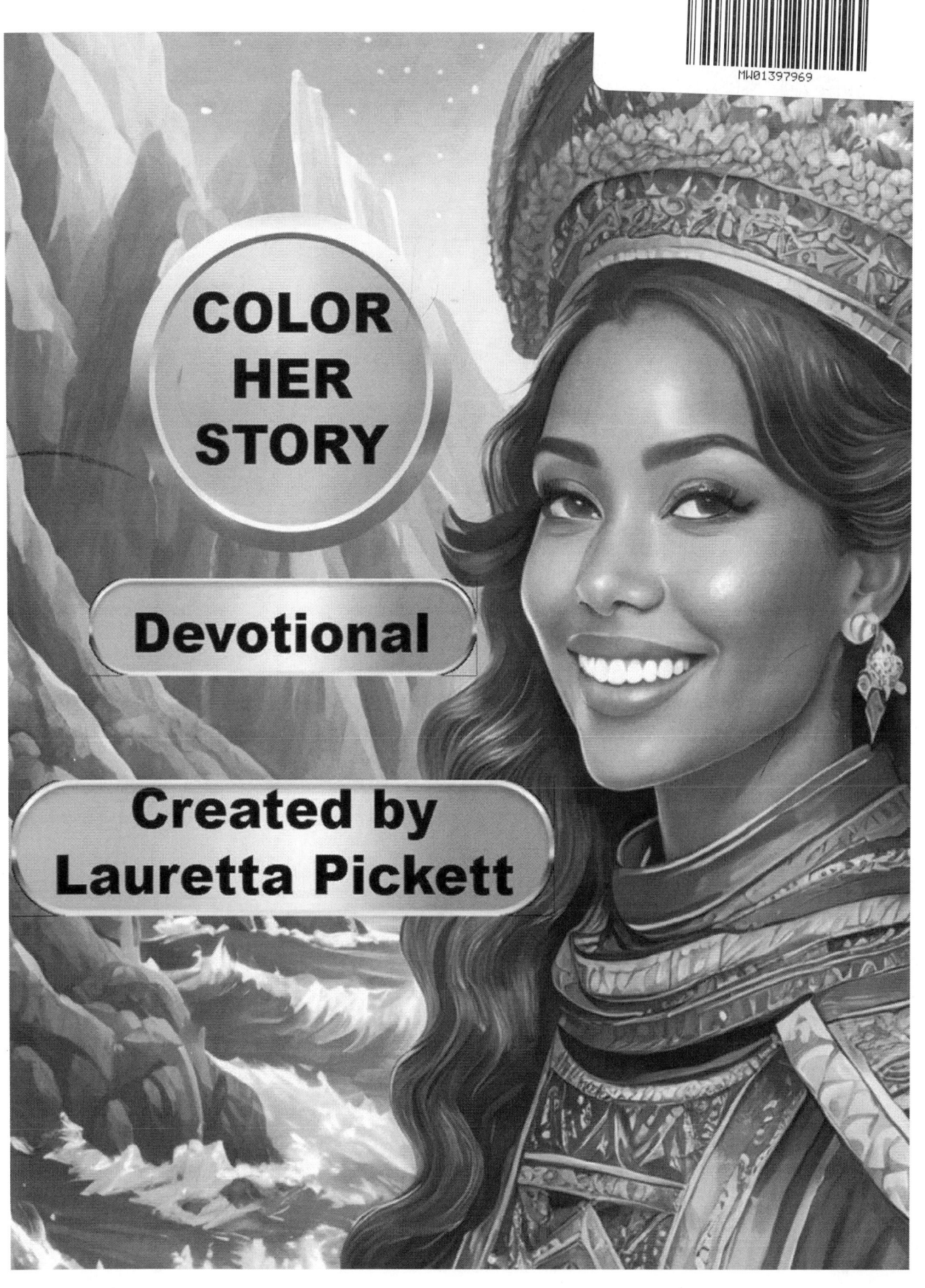

MEET THE AUTHOR

DR. LAURETTA PICKETT

"COLOR HER STORY" DEVOTIONAL

In this **Devotional, "Color Her Story,"** we will explore how words shape our thoughts, influence how we view ourselves, and ultimately determine our story.

Reflecting on my story, I recall my time at Englewood High School in Chicago. When I was caught cutting class, a police officer handcuffed me and declared, **"You will never be nothing."** During those years, I struggled with a lifestyle that included unlawful behavior, drinking, and other poor choices, further reinforcing the negativity I had internalized. It felt as if my future had been sealed by those haunting words, **"You will never be nothing."**

These words haunted me at every potential achievement. However, I eventually learned to replace those defeatist thoughts with God's powerful message: **"Be transformed by the renewing of your mind"** (Romans 12:2). Through my relationship with God and my personal development, **I overcame those obstacles, changed my story, and discovered my true purpose, helping others find their divine purpose.**

This is my story of transformation. What's Your Story?

Dr. Lauretta Pickett

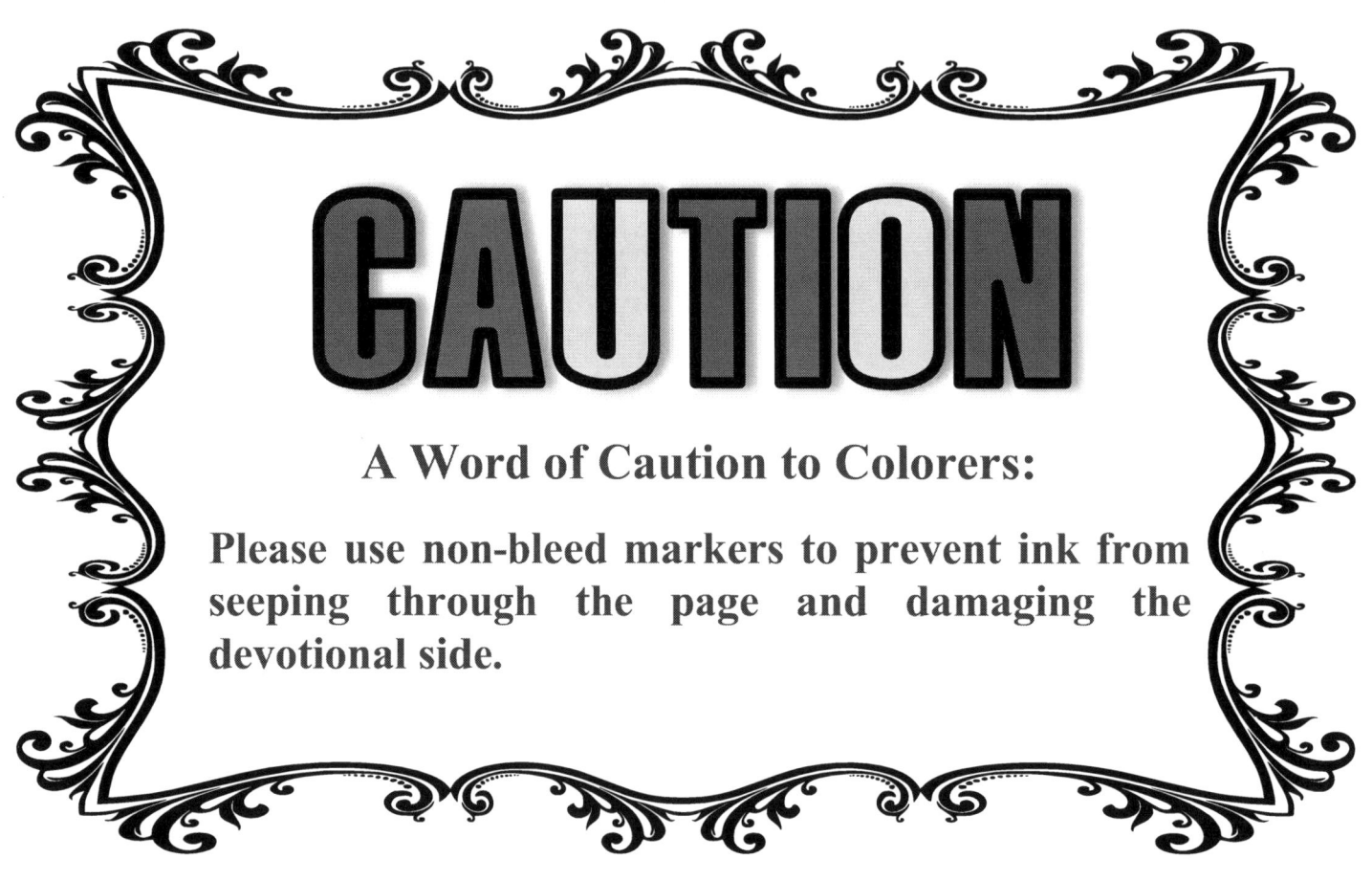

CAUTION

A Word of Caution to Colorers:

Please use non-bleed markers to prevent ink from seeping through the page and damaging the devotional side.

THE TRANSFORMATION SERIES

"Color Her Story"

Welcome to a unique devotional coloring adventure! Each page brings the stories of inspiring women to life through beautiful artwork that reflects their struggles and triumphs.

On the left side of each page, you'll find a devotional focusing on a specific word that describes her story, supported by scripture, word studies, and encouraging affirmations. **On the right side of each page,** enjoy a therapeutic coloring experience that allows for relaxation, stress relief, and enhancement of motor skills through precise hand movements.

This unique combination provides a space for both spiritual insight and emotional reflection, helping you connect deeply with each woman's journey while discovering your own path. Let this devotional coloring book be more than just a pastime; immerse yourself in God's word as you color and reflect on completing **her story!**

Created by
LAURETTA PICKETT

Copyright 2024 Lauretta Pickett All rights reserved.
No part of this book may be reproduced or transmitted in any form or by any means, including photo-copying.

Edited by Anthony Ambrogio

Published and printed in the United States of America. 2nd ed. November 2024

"COLOR HER STORY"

PURPOSE

"Many are the plans in a person's heart, but it is the Lord's purpose that prevails." Proverbs 19:21 (NIV)

Purpose: Our purpose matters, but God's plan is the ultimate guide. Divine purpose brings meaning and direction, guiding us through chaos and uncertainty. It transforms our actions into intentional and meaningful pursuits. It clarifies what you accept, what you refuse, and with whom you make covenants. It provides daily directions. **Do you know your God-given purpose?**

PRAYER FOR PURPOSE

God, I submit my will to Your purpose. I will choose only what aligns with Your plan for me. I will refuse anything that alters the path You've set. Guide my steps and grant me wisdom to understand my purpose in every area. I chose Your will. In Jesus' Name, Amen.

FAITH STATEMENT

DO YOU KNOW YOUR PURPOSE?

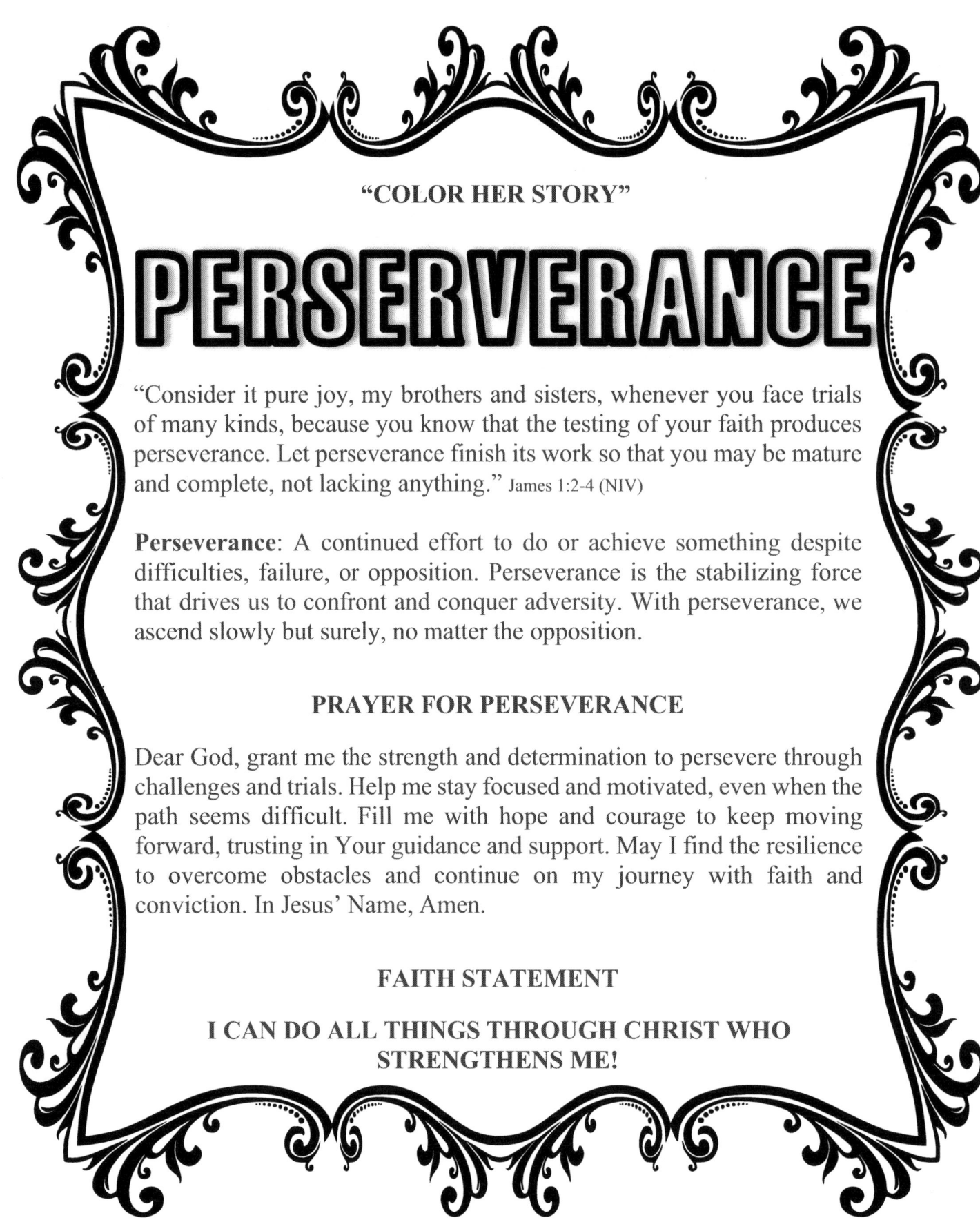

"COLOR HER STORY"

PERSERVERANCE

"Consider it pure joy, my brothers and sisters, whenever you face trials of many kinds, because you know that the testing of your faith produces perseverance. Let perseverance finish its work so that you may be mature and complete, not lacking anything." James 1:2-4 (NIV)

Perseverance: A continued effort to do or achieve something despite difficulties, failure, or opposition. Perseverance is the stabilizing force that drives us to confront and conquer adversity. With perseverance, we ascend slowly but surely, no matter the opposition.

PRAYER FOR PERSEVERANCE

Dear God, grant me the strength and determination to persevere through challenges and trials. Help me stay focused and motivated, even when the path seems difficult. Fill me with hope and courage to keep moving forward, trusting in Your guidance and support. May I find the resilience to overcome obstacles and continue on my journey with faith and conviction. In Jesus' Name, Amen.

FAITH STATEMENT

I CAN DO ALL THINGS THROUGH CHRIST WHO STRENGTHENS ME!

"COLOR HER STORY"

DREAMER

"Joseph had a dream, and when he told it to his brothers, they hated him all the more." Genesis 37:5 (NIV)

Dreamer: A dreamer is fueled by visions of what can be, seeing beyond limitations and drawing inspiration to shape reality. Despite being misunderstood, like Joseph, dreamers remain confirmed by their vision, not by others' opinions.

PRAYER FOR THE DREAMER

God, I'm opening my heart to welcome Your dreams and guidance. I'm sorry for neglecting the dreams and direction You gave me in the past, and I promise to seek insight to understand Your thoughts better. Please give me wisdom and courage to make every dream come true. Lead my steps and connect me with the people that are sent to help fulfill Your purpose for my life. In Jesus' name, Amen.

FAITH STATEMENT

"A DREAMER CAN ALWAYS DREAM AGAIN."

"COLOR HER STORY"
VISIONARY

"Where there is no vision, the people perish: but he that keep the law, happy is he." Proverbs 29:18 (KJV)

Visionaries have the ability to perceive God's purpose and align their personal visions with unwavering faith. These individuals can look into the murky waters of life and identify the paths of truth and destiny that help shape their future. When a visionary aligns their mindset, emotions, and spirit with faith, they effectively bring every vision to life.

PRAYER FOR THE VISIONARY

God, thank You for giving me free will. I let go of any desires and ambitions that go against Your will. I release any visions that might block Your purpose for my life. Please open my eyes to see Your plans. Show me the right path, as I choose to follow Your will. In Jesus' name, Amen.

FAITH STATEMENT

VISION REVEALS TOMORROW'S PATH TODAY

"COLOR HER STORY"

EMPOWERED

"Now unto him that is able to do exceeding abundantly above all that we ask or think, according to the power that worketh in us…"
Ephesians 3:20 (KJV)

Empowered: Personal empowerment means having the confidence and authority to act. It involves cultivating inner strength and confidence in your abilities and decisions.

Divine empowerment encompasses all of heavenly authority, granting strength from God. It enables individuals to achieve beyond their natural capacity through faith and Heavenly support.

PRAYER FOR EMPOWERMENT

Empower me with courage and wisdom as I face each day. Empower me to pursue my dreams and the resilience to overcome challenges. In Jesus' Name, Amen.

FAITH STATEMENT

GOD WILL FINISH WHAT HE HAS BEGUN IN ME

"COLOR HER STORY"

COMMITTED

"Commit your way to the Lord; trust in Him, and He will do this."
Psalm 37:5 (NIV)

Commitment means sticking with someone or something through thick and thin until everything is settled and secure. It helps us push through tough times and builds deep trust in relationships. However, taking on false responsibilities can lead to commitments where only the other party benefits, much like casting your pearls before swine. It's important to focus on commitments that genuinely support and enrich both your life and the lives of those involved.

PRAYER FOR COMMITMENT

God, I commit myself to You above everyone and everything. I dedicate my actions to reflect the behavior of a daughter of the King. I also commit to the relationships around me and strive to be a covenant keeper. I surrender my will to Yours, trusting that You are committed to bringing success to my life. In Jesus' Name, Amen.

FAITH STATEMENT

I AM COMMITTED TO THE WILL OF GOD, ABOVE MY OWN

"COLOR HER STORY"

SECRETS

"For God will bring every deed into judgment, including every hidden thing, whether it is good or evil." Ecclesiastes 12:14 (NIV)

Secrets live in shadows, guarding stories we're afraid to reveal due to fear of exposure. Sometimes, we hide our mistakes to avoid embarrassment or judgment, creating self-made prisons we mistake for safety. While some secrets become vows we honor, if they burden us, we should cast these cares on the Lord, and seek counsel.

In other cases, secrets are used to deceive and mislead, becoming tools of manipulation. When kept in confidence, secrets can be a sign of integrity, but we pray that those meant to deceive will be uncovered.

PRAYER FOR SECRETS

Lord, search the hidden places within me and grant me peace from the shame of my past mistakes. Release me from the pain of secrets and guide me with Your light of truth. In Jesus' Name, Amen.

FAITH STATEMENT

I WILL DWELL IN THE SECRET PLACE OF THE MOST HIGH GOD

"COLOR HER STORY"

REGRET

"Forget the former things; do not dwell on the past. See, I am doing a new thing! Now it springs up; do you not perceive it? I am making a way in the wilderness and streams in the wasteland." Isaiah 43:18-19 (NIV)

Regret: A feeling of sadness, or disappointment over something that is in your past that you cannot change. While repentance acknowledges wrongdoing, it is not a sentence of bondage to your past. Regret is the echo of missed opportunities and choices resonating in the corridors of your memory, trapped by actions or words you cannot change or repay. Forgive yourself and others, make better decisions, and turn regret into lessons you will never forget.

PRAYER FOR REGRET

Heavenly Father, I release all regrets for anything I have done or failed to do. I seek freedom from everything that's burdened me. I forgive myself and others and choose to live regret free. Open new doors, and let my regrets become stepping stones to achieve heights I have never known. In Jesus' name, Amen.

FAITH STATEMENT

REGRET TEACHES WHILE FAITH REBUILDS

"COLOR HER STORY"

FRIEND

"A friend loves at all times, and a brother is born for adversity."
Proverbs 17:17 (NIV)

Friend: A friend shares the journeys of life. A friend will never leave you even when you are wrong. They may not agree but will answer every time you call, even in adversity. If you find yourself without a friend, show yourself to be friendly and seek the awesome companionship of friendship. Woe to the person who fails alone; there will be no one to pick them up. Friends stand as pillars of unyielding support; their presence is a comforting pillow through trials and triumphs alike.

PRAYER FOR FRIENDS

I pray to be a good friend. God, please send more godly friends into my life, so we can share in You and with each other. May we build trust, love, and enjoy a wonderful life together! In Jesus' Name, Amen.

FAITH STATEMENT

A FRIEND STAYS CLOSE AT ALL TIMES

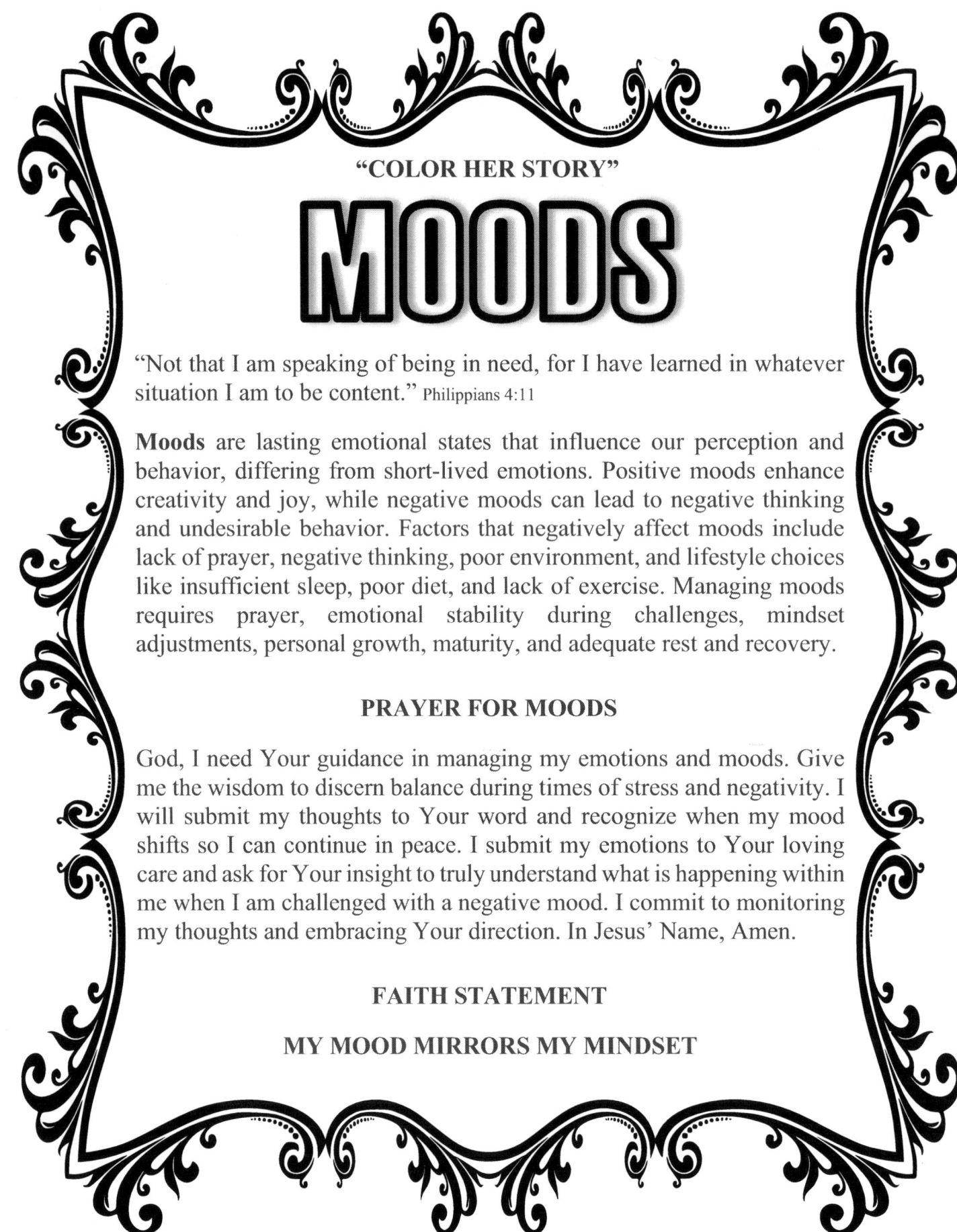

"COLOR HER STORY"

MOODS

"Not that I am speaking of being in need, for I have learned in whatever situation I am to be content." Philippians 4:11

Moods are lasting emotional states that influence our perception and behavior, differing from short-lived emotions. Positive moods enhance creativity and joy, while negative moods can lead to negative thinking and undesirable behavior. Factors that negatively affect moods include lack of prayer, negative thinking, poor environment, and lifestyle choices like insufficient sleep, poor diet, and lack of exercise. Managing moods requires prayer, emotional stability during challenges, mindset adjustments, personal growth, maturity, and adequate rest and recovery.

PRAYER FOR MOODS

God, I need Your guidance in managing my emotions and moods. Give me the wisdom to discern balance during times of stress and negativity. I will submit my thoughts to Your word and recognize when my mood shifts so I can continue in peace. I submit my emotions to Your loving care and ask for Your insight to truly understand what is happening within me when I am challenged with a negative mood. I commit to monitoring my thoughts and embracing Your direction. In Jesus' Name, Amen.

FAITH STATEMENT

MY MOOD MIRRORS MY MINDSET

"COLOR HER STORY"

WORRY

"Do not be anxious about anything, but in every situation, by prayer and petition, with thanksgiving, present your requests to God. And the peace of God, which transcends all understanding, will guard your hearts and your minds in Christ Jesus." Philippians 4:6-7 (NIV)

Worry: A state of anxiety and uncertainty over actual or potential problems. Worry is the restless cycle of fear of areas we cannot control or are too afraid to confront. Worry churns beneath the surface of uncertainty's murky waters, hindering the stability that is rightly yours. Worry is a waste of time and can never be productive.

PRAYER FOR WORRY

God, I need Your help when my heart feels overwhelmed by worry and anxiety. What I cannot control I will surrender to You and cast those burden on You, for You care for me. Help me to understand how fear and anxiety expose my limitation and reveal Your strength. In Jesus' Name, Amen.

FAITH STATEMENT

I WILL CAST MY CARES ON YOU, FOR YOU CARE FOR ME

"COLOR HER STORY"

FEAR

"God has not given us a spirit of fear, but of power and of love and of a sound mind." 2 Timothy 1:7 (KJV)

Fear, whether arising from internal insecurities or external challenges, is not given by God. God provides us with a spirit of power, love, and a sound mind. Internal fears often stem from our own insecurities and mental images, while external fears may come from intimidating forces or situations. Embracing God's love, power, and clear thinking helps us overcome the torment of fear.

PRAYER FOR FEAR

Dear Lord, I seek Your peace to remove fear from my heart. I know fear is not from You, so I ask for Your presence to shine a light brighter than the fear I am experiencing. Give me strength and understanding to overcome fear, replacing it with power, love, and a sound mind. I will remember that, with You, I am never alone. In Jesus' Name, Amen.

FAITH STATEMENT

FEAR TREMBLES BEFORE FAITH

"COLOR HER STORY"
ANGER

"In your anger do not sin": Do not let the sun go down while you are still angry, and do not give the devil a foothold. Ephesians 4:26-27 (NIV)

Anger is a powerful emotion fueled by unresolved problems and feelings of unfairness. It often pushes us to act, but, if not controlled, it can lead to regret. While anger is sometimes justified when it's righteous indignation, it's important to manage our anger with repentance and discipline. It can also reveal a need for healing from past hurts. By understanding anger, we can transform it into a source of positive change rather than letting it dominate us.

PRAYER FOR ANGER

Holding onto anger is like drinking poison and expecting the other person to die. When I am angry, help me to remember that the root cause is often unresolved issues beyond my control. Lord, help me release this anger so I don't harm others or change who I am. Thank you for reminding me in your word that anger is natural but must be released so I don't sin. In Jesus' Name, Amen.

FAITH STATEMENT

ANGER IS ONE LETTER SHORT OF DANGER

"COLOR HER STORY"

HURT

"The Lord is close to the brokenhearted and saves those who are crushed in spirit." Psalm 34:18 (NIV)

Hurt: Hurt yields its power with sharp precision, etching deep marks within the spirit, soul, and body with undue heaviness. It dwells in moments of injury, whether physical, emotional, or spiritual. We should immediately release hurt, realizing that hurting people hurt people. If a hurting person does not let go of hurt, the final result is that the hurting person becomes the offender.

PRAYER FOR HURT

God, I ask your help to heal me from hurt. I surrender my right to hold the wrong that was done to me, and choose to be free through forgiveness. In Jesus' Name, Amen.

FAITH STATEMENT

HURT IS OVERCOME BY MY DECISION TO WALK IN LOVE

"COLOR HER STORY"

ABANDONED

"Can a mother forget the baby at her breast and have no compassion on the child she has borne? Though she may forget, I will not forget you! See, I have engraved you on the palms of my hands; your walls are ever before me." Isaiah 49:15-16 (NIV)

Abandoned: To feel abandoned is to encounter echoes of departure and emptiness. Despite the solitary silence, abandonment can also serve as fertile ground for rebirth and independence. Within its walls lies the potential for transformation and new life. In the will of God, things may not always feel good, but all things work together for the good of those who love God and are called according to His purpose.

PRAYER FOR THE ABANDONED

God, I pray for healing and deliverance from abandonment, knowing I cannot force anyone to stay if they choose to leave. You are the one who promised you will never leave or forsake me. Therefore, I release any responsibilities of those who did not stay, and I forgive them. In Jesus' Name, Amen.

FAITH STATEMENT

ABANDONED PATHS CAN LEAD SOMEWHERE NEW

"COLOR HER STORY"

REVENGE

"Dearly beloved, avenge not yourselves, but rather give place unto wrath: for it is written, Vengeance is mine; I will repay, saith the Lord."
Romans 12:19 (KJV)

Revenge: Revenge is about wanting to hurt someone because they hurt you. It can feel powerful initially, but it often leaves you empty. Choosing forgiveness frees you from bitterness, and patience is key. Trust that God's justice will ultimately prevail.

PRAYER FOR REVENGE

God, I trust you to avenge any wrongs against me. I refuse to become like those who hurt me. I trust in your justice. In Jesus' Name, Amen.

FAITH STATEMENT

I TRUST GOD TO AVENGE ME!

"COLOR HER STORY"
WRONGED

"And we know that all things work together for good to them that love God, to them who are the called according to his purpose." Romans 8:28 (KJV)

Wronged: Feeling 'wronged' means experiencing unfair or unjust treatment, leading to emotions like anger, sadness, or frustration, often due to betrayal, deception, or a breach of trust. Women in particular might seek justice for being wronged, simply for being a woman. Let wisdom guide you toward a future unburdened by the past.

PRAYER FOR JUSTICE

God, I release any anger from being done wrong. I ask for healing in my heart and understanding of what I should do in this season as I wait on you. In Jesus' Name, Amen.

FAITH STATEMENT

WHEN WRONGED, SEEK WISDOM, NOT REVENGE

"COLOR HER STORY"

FAITHFUL

"She is clothed with strength and dignity; she can laugh at the days to come. She speaks with wisdom, and faithful instruction is on her tongue."
Proverbs 31:25-26 (NIV)

A **Faithful** woman: In the heart of every woman lies unwavering strength, a beacon of resilience that shines through every promise kept and every challenge faced. Faithful to God, her family, and friends, she embodies a steadfast spirit that empowers and inspires, leading with grace and integrity.

PRAYER FOR FAITHFULNESS

God, I acknowledge that my faithfulness is not dependent on the actions of others. In moments where I have not been faithful, I seek Your forgiveness and guidance to become more supportive. I will also ask forgiveness to anyone I have not been faithful to. In Jesus' Name, Amen.

FAITH STATEMENT

FAITH SHOWS THE FUTURE WHEN IT'S DARK AHEAD

"COLOR HER STORY"

TEACHER

"Instruct the wise, and they will be wiser still; teach the righteous, and they will add to their learning." Proverbs 9:9 (NIV)

Teacher: Women educators often nurture their families first and extend this care to their communities, sharing their wisdom and knowledge. Even in areas like business and ministry, where they have faced opposition, they continue to uplift others. Despite challenges due to gender, women educators progress with the aim not to compete but to help complete, enriching everyone around them with knowledge and wisdom. Their influence stirs lifelong learning and personal growth, nurturing both minds and spirits.

PRAYER FOR THE TEACHER

God, I pray for the women educators who dedicate themselves to nurturing souls and spirits with wisdom and care. May they be blessed with strength, support, and grace as they enrich their families and communities, inspiring everyone they teach. In Jesus' Name, Amen.

FAITH STATEMENT

"EVERY STUDENT SEARCHES FOR A TEACHER"

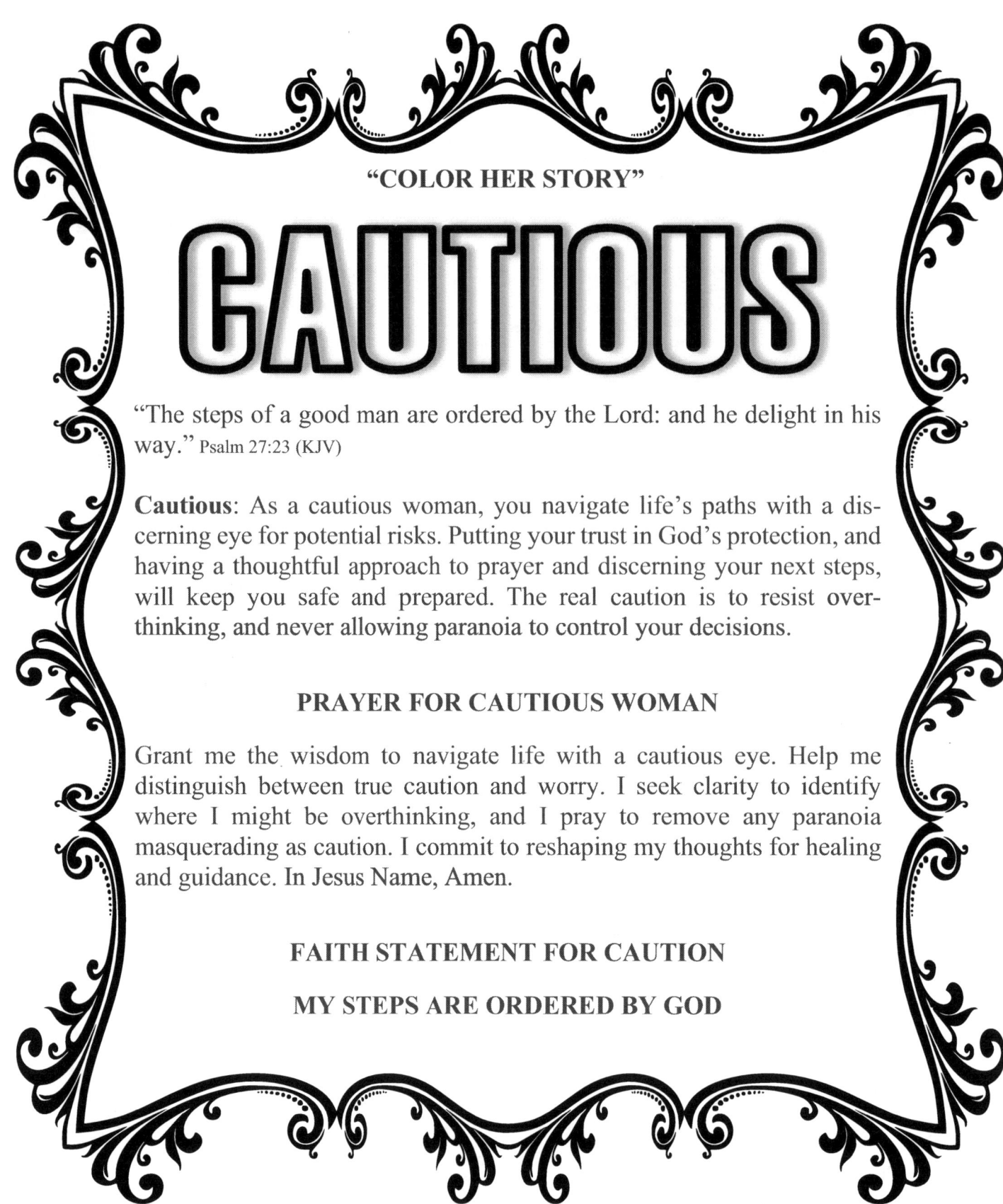

"COLOR HER STORY"

CAUTIOUS

"The steps of a good man are ordered by the Lord: and he delight in his way." Psalm 27:23 (KJV)

Cautious: As a cautious woman, you navigate life's paths with a discerning eye for potential risks. Putting your trust in God's protection, and having a thoughtful approach to prayer and discerning your next steps, will keep you safe and prepared. The real caution is to resist overthinking, and never allowing paranoia to control your decisions.

PRAYER FOR CAUTIOUS WOMAN

Grant me the wisdom to navigate life with a cautious eye. Help me distinguish between true caution and worry. I seek clarity to identify where I might be overthinking, and I pray to remove any paranoia masquerading as caution. I commit to reshaping my thoughts for healing and guidance. In Jesus Name, Amen.

FAITH STATEMENT FOR CAUTION

MY STEPS ARE ORDERED BY GOD

"COLOR HER STORY"

ASSERTIVE

"The wicked flee when no man pursueth: but the righteous are bold as a lion." Proverbs 28:1 (KJV)

Assertiveness involves confidently and clearly communicating your ideas and needs, without aggression or arrogance. This courage comes from living a righteous and upright life. When you act with integrity, you naturally become assertive, like a lion who moves with boldness and assurance. It is about expressing yourself with clarity and intention, not being afraid to show your strengths while maintaining respect for others.

PRAYER FOR THE ASSERTIVE

God, help me move forward in confidence toward the vision You placed in me. I want to move with boldness but never forget to humble myself and keep my heart open for Your examination, to expose any pride or arrogance. I want to walk with assertiveness while I remember to respect those around me. In Jesus' Name, Amen

FAITH STATEMENT

I DOMINATE FEAR BY WALKING BY FAITH

"COLOR HER STORY"
WEEPING

"Weeping may endure for a night, but joy cometh in the morning."
Psalm 30:5 (KJV)

Weeping: Crying is a natural way to release emotions, whether from pain or joy. In some traditions, tears are treasured. For example, women once collected tears in bottles for loved ones at war, each tear symbolizing a moment of pain for them leaving or joy for their return. However, it's important to distinguish between temporary mourning and prolonged weeping, as persistent crying may indicate depression or the need for deliverance. Recognizing the importance of seeking help, whatever the problem, can open the door to healing and reveal a new story, filled with faith, that joy comes in the morning.

PRAYER FOR WEEPING

"May I be blessed with the strength and peace to face whatever emotions come my way. The days that tears fill my eyes, for whatever reason. may they bring healing and a reminder I am human even when I want to be brave. God, reveal to me if what I am dealing with is too hard for me; I will seek support. Guide me through the valleys, decisions, and the murky waters of unstable emotions and help me find resilience and guidance in every step I take. In Jesus' Name, Amen.

FAITH STATEMENT

GOD HAS BOTTLED EVERY ONE OF MY TEARS

"COLOR HER STORY"

STRATEGIC

"For which of you, intending to build a tower, sit not down first, and count the cost, whether he have sufficient to finish it?" Luke 14:28

Strategic thinking is a woman's secret weapon in fulfilling her purpose. The average woman multitasks daily; therefore, it's crucial for her to pause and plan her next steps to avoid exhaustion and becoming overwhelmed. Strategy acts as a personal support system, empowering her to accomplish goals and establish discipline, which creates a calmness in her life. Use strategy to uplift, not to manipulate those around you. Embrace a strategic mindset to achieve your greatest potential.

PRAYER FOR STRATEGY

God, I need strategy to understand my next steps, My steps are ordered by you, and I need to understand your order. When I am dealing with challenges in family, business, relationships, or finances, I need your wisdom. I will submit to you and refuse to walk in manipulation, I will listen for your voice to follow your guidance, In Jesus' Name, Amen.

FAITH STATEMENT

STRATEGY REQUIRES THOUGHT BEFORE MOVEMENT

COLOR HER STORY"

BRAVE

"So do not fear, for I am with you; do not be dismayed, for I am your God." Isaiah 41:10 (NIV)

Bravery isn't about being fearless but about choosing strength in the face of fear. For women, it means speaking your truth, pursuing your dreams, and confronting challenges head-on. Embrace bravery by standing up for yourself and others, pushing boundaries, and recognizing your worth. Bravery balances vulnerability and perseverance, daring to step into the unknown without arrogance or passivity.

PRAYER FOR THE BRAVE

Lord, many see me as brave, but I ask you for strength. For, without you, I can do nothing. Thank you for protecting me and giving me the confidence to know that in every battle I never fight alone! In Jesus' Name, Amen.

FAITH STATEMENT

BRAVERY IS A BALANCING ACT

"COLOR HER STORY"

HARDNESS

"Thou therefore endure hardness, as a good soldier of Jesus Christ."
2 Timothy 2:3 (KJV)

Hardness: A woman often develops hardness as a protective shield against life's challenges and experiences of adversity and struggle. She uses this self-made armor of hardness to help her survive and face difficulties. However, she must allow hardness to be broken to create deeper connections. She must let go; it's her path to freedom, allowing others to see a healed woman who has longed to be seen and understood.

PRAYER FOR HARDNESS

God, search my heart, and, no matter the reason for the hardness of my heart, I want to let go of this internal prison of my heart. I forgive everyone who hurt me, and I make a decision to give up my choice of unforgiveness: I forgive. In Jesus' Name, Amen.

FAITH STATEMENT

HEAL YOURSELF BY LETTING GO

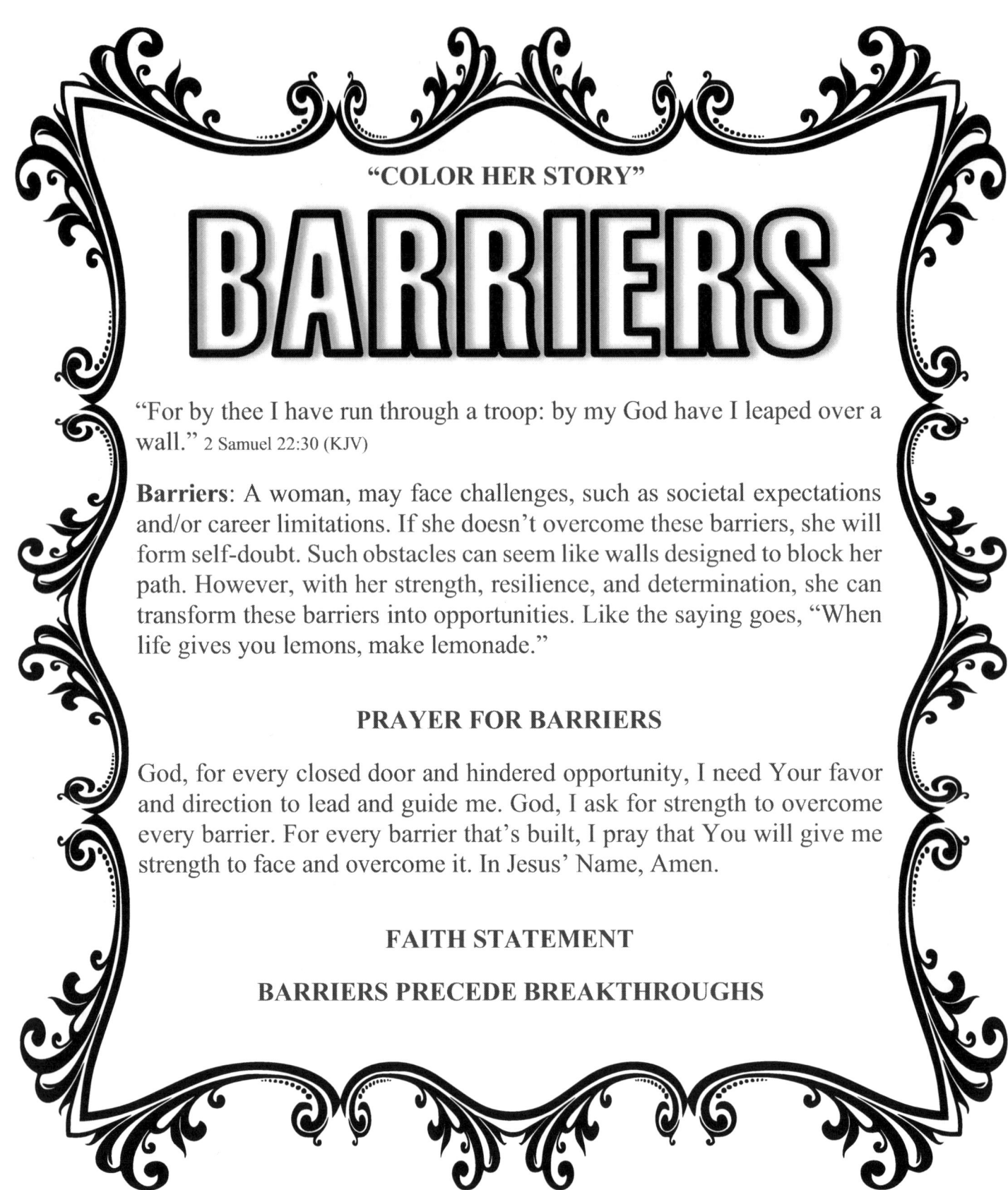

"COLOR HER STORY"

BARRIERS

"For by thee I have run through a troop: by my God have I leaped over a wall." 2 Samuel 22:30 (KJV)

Barriers: A woman, may face challenges, such as societal expectations and/or career limitations. If she doesn't overcome these barriers, she will form self-doubt. Such obstacles can seem like walls designed to block her path. However, with her strength, resilience, and determination, she can transform these barriers into opportunities. Like the saying goes, "When life gives you lemons, make lemonade."

PRAYER FOR BARRIERS

God, for every closed door and hindered opportunity, I need Your favor and direction to lead and guide me. God, I ask for strength to overcome every barrier. For every barrier that's built, I pray that You will give me strength to face and overcome it. In Jesus' Name, Amen.

FAITH STATEMENT

BARRIERS PRECEDE BREAKTHROUGHS

"COLOR HER STORY"

ISOLATION

"Two are better than one, because they have a good return for their labor: If either of them falls down, one can help the other up. But pity anyone who falls and has no one to help them up." Ecclesiastes 4:9-10 (NIV)

Isolation, whether emotional or physical, can bring challenges. Emotional isolation may leave you feeling lonely even when surrounded by others, while physical isolation can result from separating yourself due to hurt or health issues. Instead, consider transforming this isolation into a time of consecration, dedicating it to prayer and nurturing your inner strength and faith. By changing your mindset, you can begin building relationships that support you during times of feeling alone and isolation.

PRAYER FOR ISOLATION

Lord, empower me to break free of the walls built from fear and rejection. These barriers, once meant to protect, now confine my spirit. Guide me to shed these limitations and embrace the abundant life You desire for me. In Jesus' Name, Amen.

FAITH STATEMENT

ISOLATION IS THE LONELINESS OF ONE'S HEART

"COLOR HER STORY"

PATIENCE

"But let patience have her perfect work, that ye may be perfect and entire, wanting nothing." James 1:4 (KJV)

Patience allows a person to endure challenges without frustration and to make thoughtful decisions. It gives us the ability to pause, reflect, and adapt, preventing impulsive reactions. Some may avoid praying for patience, fearing it might bring trials, but this is misguided. Patience is a virtue for us as women to empower us to complete what we start. Patience gives us an opportunity to rest and recover to overcome obstacles gracefully.

PRAYER FOR PATIENCE

"Dear God, sometimes I struggle with waiting, and I need Your help to learn patience. Please help me understand why sometimes I have difficulty trusting You, even though You have never let me down. Remind me that my impatience is a sign that I need to let patience have her perfect work. In Jesus' Name, Amen.

FAITH STATEMENT

PATIENCE IS HOW WE ACT WHILE WAITING

"COLOR HER STORY"

COURAGEOUS

"Have I not commanded you? Be strong and courageous. Do not be afraid; do not be discouraged, for the Lord your God will be with you wherever you go." Joshua 1:9

Courageous: Courageousness involves facing fear, danger, or adversity with strength and determination. It's about stepping outside your comfort zone and taking action in the face of challenges. Being courageous doesn't mean the absence of fear, but rather the ability to move forward despite it.

PRAYER FOR THE COURAGEOUS

Dear Lord, grant me the courage to face fears and overcome adversity. Help me to step outside my comfort zone and take action, even when it's difficult. I pray to never forget that courage is not the absence of fear but the willingness to move forward despite it. I trust you hear my pray. In Jesus' Name, Amen.

FAITH STATEMENT

COURAGE IS COMMITMENT, DESPITE FEAR

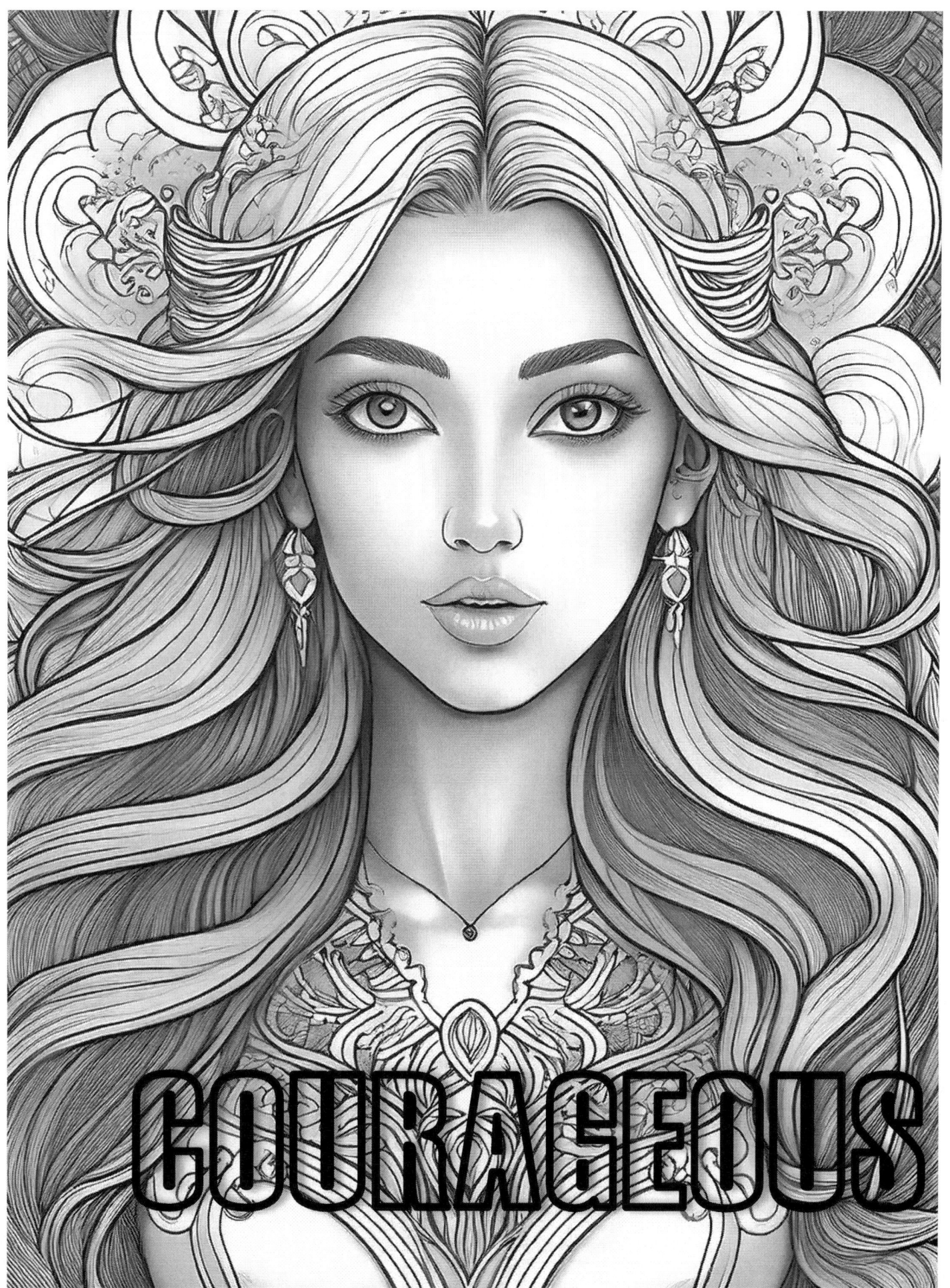

"COLOR HER STORY"

CONCERNED

"Peace I leave with you; my peace I give you. I do not give to you as the world gives. Do not let your hearts be troubled and do not be afraid."
John 14:27 (NIV)

Concerned: A woman's concern allows her to care deeply about the well-being of others, showing empathy and compassion. However, when we are overwhelmed with concern, it creates worry that leaves a women drained, because she is always thinking about how to fix things for others. While being concerned is a sign of empathy and compassion, finding a balance is crucial to avoid burning out and to ensure you're in the best shape to help others but not forget about God and yourself.

PRAYER FOR THE CONCERNED

Grant me the strength to balance my care for others with the care for myself. Help me to recognize when my concern becomes overwhelming, and guide me back to a place of peace, rest, and recovery. In Jesus' Name, Amen.

FAITH STATEMENT

CONCERN IS COMPASSION IN ACTION

"COLOR HER STORY"

RESENTFUL

"Hatred stirs up conflict, but love covers over all wrongs."
Proverbs 10:12 (NIV)

Resentful: When Mrs. Resentful's husband abandoned her and their children, her world seemed to crumble. She financially struggled, while her husband started a new family, caring for children who weren't even his own, neglecting the ones he left behind.

The sting of betrayal deepened her resentment, But then she asked God for forgiveness. She decided Mrs. Resentful was not who she wanted to be. She sought support and found her voice. Shedding layers of pain, she began emerging like a butterfly from its cocoon, rewriting her story.

PRAYER FOR BEING RESENTFUL

Dear God, if there is any resentment in my heart, please reveal it to me. I surrender my desire for revenge against those who have hurt me. Cleanse my heart, Lord, so that I may be free of bitterness. Fill me with peace and forgiveness. I pray In Jesus' Name, Amen.

FAITH STATEMENT

RESENTMENT IS SELF-POISONING

"COLOR HER STORY"

INSECURITY

"God is our refuge and strength, an ever-present help in trouble."
Psalm 46:1 (NIV)

Insecurity often involves a lack of confidence or a sense of self-doubt in various areas. It can stem from past experiences, comparisons with others, or feelings of inadequacy. To overcome insecurity, recognize your unique strengths and achievements. Surround yourself with supportive people who uplift you. Remember you are enough; there is no one in the world who can truly be YOU.

PRAYER FOR INSECURITY

Dear God, please fill me with confidence and courage. Help me to see my worth and trust in your plan. Guide me to overcome my fears and embrace your love. In Jesus' Name, Amen.

FAITH STATEMENT

INSECURITIES WHISPER LIES ABOUT OUR IDENTITY

"COLOR HER STORY"

DYNAMIC

"For the word of God is quick and powerful and sharper than any two-edged sword" Hebrews 4:12 (KJV)

Dynamic: A dynamic woman fills a room with her presence; her very essence demands attention. Her inner confidence radiates stability and strength. Her eyes are captivating, not just because of their color, but because they reflect resilience as she listens intently to every word you say. What's truly inspiring is how her powerful presence uplifts everyone she meets, knowing who she is while never forgetting those around her.

PRAYER FOR THE DYNAMIC WOMAN

God, as a confident woman, I seek not only to strengthen myself but also to support those women who are still finding their confidence. Grant me wisdom to assist and uplift them while they are facing any fears and insecurities. I pray for divine connections and support in her life. In Jesus' Name, Amen.

FAITH STATEMENT

MY CONFIDENCE IS BASED ON WHAT I BELIEVE

"COLOR HER STORY"

SERENITY

"Thou wilt keep him in perfect peace, whose mind is stayed on thee: because he trust in thee." Isaiah 26:3 (KJV)

Serenity for a woman is finding a deep sense of calm and strength within herself in the midst of life's demands and emotions. It's the quiet space where she can let go of perfectionism, embrace stillness, and be present. By nurturing this inner peace, she gains clarity and resilience, inspiring herself and others with a quiet confidence.

PRAYER FOR SERENITY

When I need peace, I will run to prayer—the place of peace and calmness. I ask for the safety of trusting You and seeing my life out of Your eyes. In Jesus' Name, Amen.

FAITH STATEMENT

SERENITY IS A SACRED PLACE

"COLOR HER STORY"

THOUGHTFUL

"Let each of you look not only to his own interests, but also to the interests of others." Philippians 2:4

Thoughtful: A thoughtful woman is a person who consistently shows empathy and care for others. She listens attentively and offers genuine support, often anticipating needs before they're expressed. Her actions, guided by compassion, create an environment where others feel valued and respected. Through small gestures of kindness and thoughtful reflection, she uplifts those around her, leaving a positive impact on everyone she meets.

PRAYER FOR THE THOUGHTFUL

God, I pray for the thoughtful people around the world, who think of others and strengthen them with actions and words of encouragement. I pray that every thoughtful person will reap what that have sown in others' lives. In Jesus' Name, Amen.

FAITH STATEMENT

THOUGHTFULNESS MIRRORS THE HEART

"COLOR HER STORY"

DELILAH

"Better to live on a corner of the roof than share a house with a quarrelsome wife." Proverbs 21:9 (NIV)

Delilah was known for her beauty and ability to manipulate Samson, leading him to reveal the secret of his strength, which was his covenant with God. This desire for control and wealth is still common today. However, change is possible. God offers a way to transform by healing the heart from bitterness, selfishness, and the need for revenge. Delilah simply needs to submit her heart to God for true healing and deliverance from control and greed.

PRAYER FOR DELILAH

This prayer is for the woman who wishes to change from manipulation rooted in greed and control. You might think, "I want to change, but who will trust me?" The requirements are not based on your past, but on repentance and restitution where needed. I pray for your transformation, In Jesus' Name, Amen.

FAITH STATEMENT

BEAUTY IS TO BE ADMIRED NOT FOR SEDUCTION

"COLOR HER STORY"

EXPECTATION

"For surely there is an end; and thine expectation shall not be cut off."
Proverbs 23:18 (KJV)

Expectation is the thrilling anticipation of what has yet to unfold. It's like a pregnant woman who, despite not yet seeing her baby, has faith for what she can't see. There's an unseen world where things materialize beyond our view, affirming that we can "call those things that be not as though they were." Embrace this journey, knowing that your expectation will not be cut off.

PRAYER FOR EXPECTATION

May hope fill my heart and guide my path as I wait with patience and trust. Grant me the strength to nurture my expectations with faith, confident that my expectation determines my results. In Jesus' Name, Amen.

FAITH STATEMENT

MY EXPECTATION WILL NOT BE CUT OFF

"COLOR HER STORY"

TENACIOUS

"But let patience have her perfect work, that ye may be perfect and entire, wanting nothing." James 1:4 (KJV)

Tenacious: Being tenacious means you never give up, tirelessly pursuing your dreams and overcoming any obstacles with courage and strength. The Tenacious Woman will not be intimidated or hindered, especially when it comes to her family and friends; she will protect them with her life.

PRAYER FOR THE TENACIOUS WOMAN

I pray for humility for the tenacious woman, bold, supportive but sometimes forget about herself. I pray for directions to avoid pride and hastiness. In Jesus Name Amen

FAITH STATEMENT

I AM BOLD YET SENSITIVE

"COLOR HER STORY"

FORGIVE

"Do not judge, and you will not be judged. Do not condemn, and you will not be condemned. Forgive, and you will be forgiven." Luke 6:37 (NIV)

Forgiveness is a powerful act that frees you first and releases the person you're forgiving from the prison of your revenge. For women, because you incubate feelings and thoughts, embracing forgiveness is vital for spiritual, mental, physical, and emotional stability. Unforgiveness is like an invisible poison, rooted out only by repentance and forgiveness. Remember, you cannot be forgiven unless you first forgive.

PRAYER FOR FORGIVENESS

I repent for unforgiveness, knowing I have needed forgiveness just like the person I need to release. I want to let go of the belief that forgiving means the other person wins. That's when I hear your voice reminding me, "I forgave you." Thank You, Lord, for your forgiveness. In Jesus' Name, Amen.

FAITH STATEMENT

FORGIVENESS UNLOCK PRISONS

"COLOR HER STORY"

PAIN

"He heals the brokenhearted and binds up their wounds." Psalm 147:3 (NIV)

Pain signals a call for help to address a problem. Some problems can be resolved, while others require disconnection from their source. For physical pain, accept love and support. If the pain was created by your choices, change them. If others cause the pain, seek resolution; if that's not possible, find a path to freedom from pain.

PRAYER FOR PAIN

God, whatever the reason for pain in my life, it's not Your will for me to hurt. I know You understand, for You can touch any feelings I have. I ask for Your healing and comfort to remove all pain. In Jesus' Name, Amen.

FAITH STATEMENT

PAIN IS A SIGNAL FOR CHANGE

"COLOR HER STORY"

DOUBT

"Trust in the LORD with all your heart, and lean not on your own understanding." Proverbs 3:5

Doubt: Everyone faces doubt, but it's your decisions that shape your success. Doubt is your moment to pause and choose your path. Trust in yourself, and remember that every whisper of doubt can be silenced by your courage and faith. Doubt simply means "Decide!"

PRAYER FOR DOUBT

God, I need help surrendering confidently to Your will for my life. I know You hear me, and, because I know You hear me, I rest that I have the petition that I ask of You. In Jesus' Name, Amen.

FAITH STATEMENT

DOUBT IS THE WHISPER OF CHOICE

"COLOR HER STORY"

CALM

"Cast all your anxiety on him because he cares for you." 1 Peter 5:7 (NIV)

Calm: With so many demands on your time and attention, making calmness a priority is essential. While you may not always be able to escape to a serene island, your imagination can take you anywhere. You deserve those moments to step back and simply be **YOU!**

PRAYER FOR CALMNESS

God, quiet the storms within me and grant me clarity and patience in every situation I face. Surround me with Your love and protection, and guide me as I trust you every step of the way. In Jesus' name, Amen.

FAITH STATEMENT

A CALM MINDSET LEADS TO CLEAR DECISIONS

"COLOR HER STORY"

SADNESS

"The LORD is close to the brokenhearted and saves those who are crushed in spirit." Psalm 34:18 (NIV)

Sadness; Sadness is a signal from the heart, the place we hold feelings. A signal to let go, a desire for fellowship or a time to make decisions. Instead of fleeing from unfamiliar feelings, we should identify and address their causes. By understanding the reason for sadness, we can exchange it for joy.

PRAYER TO REMOVE SADNESS

Lord, I ask for help in times of sadness. Search my heart and help me understand the inner pain that is showing through sadness. You came to give me life; therefore, I want to live free from the bondage of sadness. In Jesus' Name, Amen

FAITH STATEMENT

SADNESS IS AN EMOTION FROM HEART

"COLOR HER STORY"

BOLD

"The wicked flee though no one pursues, but the righteous are as bold as a lion." (Proverbs 28:1, NIV)

BOLD

Being bold requires courage. While doubt and fear may arise, boldness allows you to act on what you know is necessary. It means staying the course, no matter the challenges, remembering your why.

PRAYER FOR BOLDNESS

God, give me the courage to be bold. I want to face fear with faith and stay true to my purpose. Guide me in acting with integrity. I want to trust You and walk in boldness so that fear will have no power over me. In Jesus' Name, Amen.

FAITH STATEMENT
BOLDNESS IS COURAGE IN ACTION

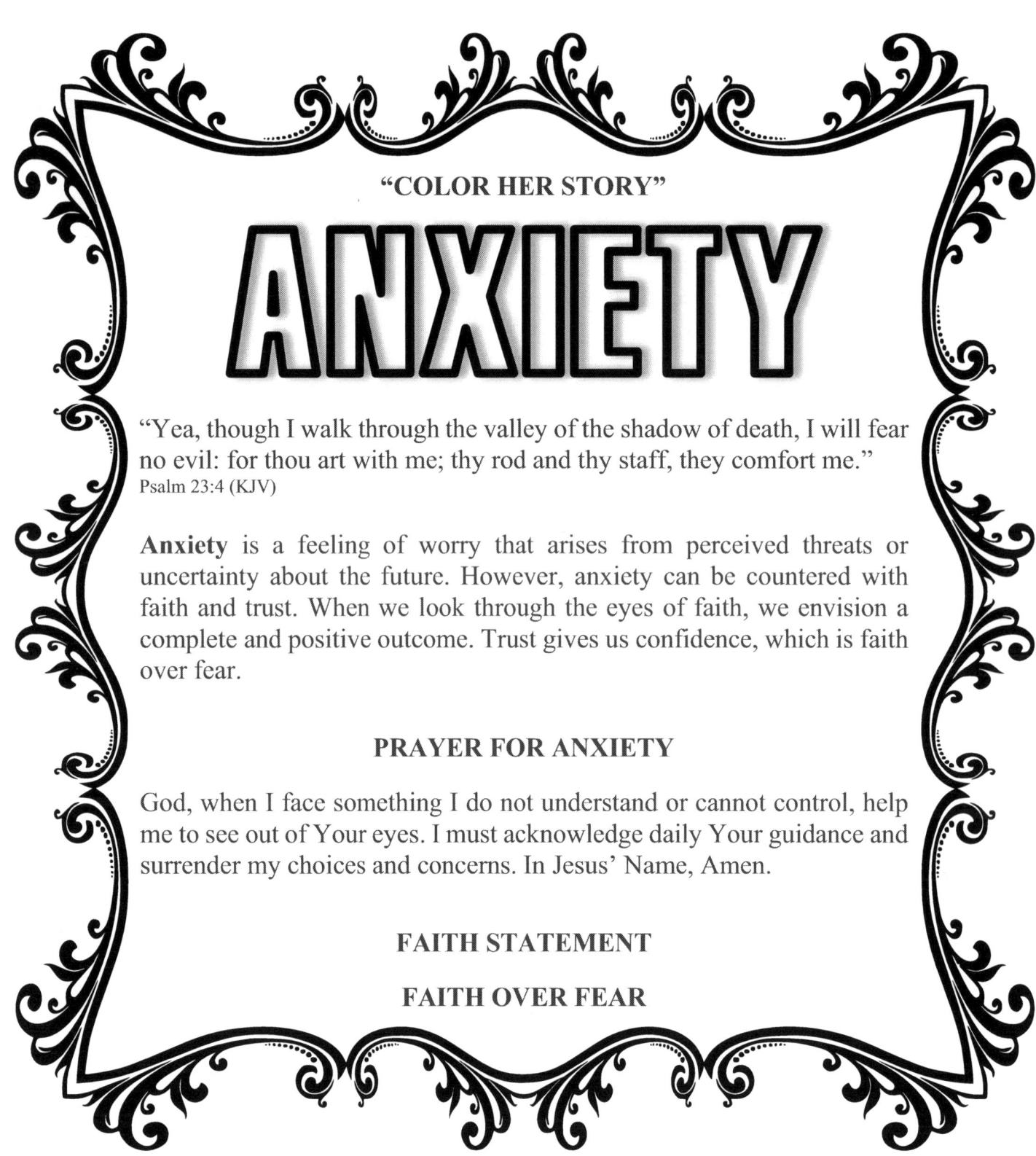

"COLOR HER STORY"

ANXIETY

"Yea, though I walk through the valley of the shadow of death, I will fear no evil: for thou art with me; thy rod and thy staff, they comfort me."
Psalm 23:4 (KJV)

Anxiety is a feeling of worry that arises from perceived threats or uncertainty about the future. However, anxiety can be countered with faith and trust. When we look through the eyes of faith, we envision a complete and positive outcome. Trust gives us confidence, which is faith over fear.

PRAYER FOR ANXIETY

God, when I face something I do not understand or cannot control, help me to see out of Your eyes. I must acknowledge daily Your guidance and surrender my choices and concerns. In Jesus' Name, Amen.

FAITH STATEMENT

FAITH OVER FEAR

"COLOR HER STORY"

LOVED

"For God so loved the world, that he gave his only begotten Son, that whosoever believeth in him should not perish, but have everlasting life."
John 3:16 (KJV)

THE VARIOUS TYPES OF LOVE

AGAPE: selfless, unconditional **LOVE**

PHILIA: love found in friendships: **LOVE**

PHILAUTIA: self-love, confidence and self-care: **LOVE**

EROS romantic love based on passion and attraction: **LOVE**

PRAGMA: long-term love in committed relationships: **LOVE**

STORGE: the special bond between parents and children: **LOVE**

LUDUS: a playful and exciting love, typical of early romance: **LOVE**

FAITH STATEMENT

"LOVE OVER EVERYTHING"

"COLOR HER STORY"

MATURE

"When I was a child, I spake as a child, I understood as a child, I thought as a child: but, when I became a man, I put away childish things."
1 Corinthians 13:11 (KJV)

Maturity and personal development are crucial for leading a stable and purpose-filled life. Maturity involves the ability to reflect on past experiences, learn from mistakes, and consistently make wise decisions. On the other hand, personal development is an ongoing process of improving one's skills, knowledge, and self-awareness. While maturity is about applying wisdom to everyday situations, personal development focuses on growing and evolving over time. We perish for a lack of knowledge.

PRAYER

Dear God, when I think of maturity, I understand it requires discipline, responsibility, and letting go of old habits. I seek Your wisdom because it can feel overwhelming at times. I am reminded that to whom much is given, much is required. Lord, I desire more in life, and I am willing to give much more in return. In Jesus' Name, Amen.

FAITH STATEMENT

I PUT AWAY CHILDISH THINGS

"COLOR HER STORY"

RESILIENT

"We are troubled on every side, yet not distressed; we are perplexed, but not in despair." 2 Corinthians 4:8 (KJV)

Resilient: A resilient woman recovers quickly from difficulties and setbacks. She is adaptable, choosing to bounce back from challenges while keeping her heart open. Even when her thoughts, relationships, and the world around her are in turmoil, she finds strength in the still, small voice of God, and returns to her original position, called resilient.

PRAYER FOR RESILIENT WOMAN

God, the days I am exhausted and need Your strength give me resilience to continue. I will look for Your help, and in Your strength I will recover and bounce back with resilience. In Jesus' Name, Amen.

FAITH STATEMENT

SHOW UP EVERY DAY

"COLOR HER STORY"

ARTIST

"And all the skilled artisans among you are to come and make everything the Lord has commanded." Exodus 35:10 (NIV)

Artist: The woman artist colors her story every day on the canvas of her imagination. She can change the course of a storm with the stroke of her pen. To truly understand her, you'd need to see through her eyes, to glimpse the world as she does. This woman transforms lives with each thought she conjures; she is a rare find, and we treasure the Creative Woman.

PRAYER FOR THE ARTIST

God, I am creative, but today the world seems less colorful. The drive to pursue anything feels far away, and I need Your help. Then I notice the beauty of the sun shining on my face, and my hands begin to paint. It's clear that my creativity truly comes from YOU. In Jesus' Name, Amen.

FAITH STATEMENT

I CAN REWRITE MY STORY

"COLOR HER STORY"

SHYNESS

"For God has not given us a spirit of fear, but of power and of love and of a sound mind." 2 Timothy 1:7 (NKJV)

Shyness is the soft hum of a heart holding back, a delicate balance of caution and vulnerability. When balanced, it becomes a reserved nature, wisely withholding thoughts until the right moment. However, unchecked shyness can create a self-made prison, causing entrapment created by our own thoughts of insecurity. It's important to remember that a shy woman is not a weak woman; she possesses a quiet strength that should not be underestimated. It's essential to celebrate the unique qualities every woman brings and embrace our individuality.

PRAYER FOR SHYNESS

I pray for the shy woman who faces a world that can often feel intimidating. Please help her uncover and appreciate the gifts and wisdom within her heart. Surround her with supportive family and friends who can remind her of her unique awesomeness. In Jesus' Name, Amen.

FAITH STATEMENT

FEAR SIGNALS RESET

"COLOR HER STORY"

MELANCHOLY

"Why, my soul, are you downcast? Why so disturbed within me? Put your hope in God, for I will yet praise him, my Savior and my God."
Psalm 42:11 (NIV)

Melancholy: Melancholy is a deep feeling of sadness and regret, reflecting on past moments you cannot change. When it arises, you must quickly decide to let these experiences transform your pain into insight.

PRAYER MELANCHOLY

When my heart is overwhelmed with thoughts of sadness, loss, and failure, I surrender these burdens to You, God. Transform my emptiness into joy and laughter, as only You can. In Jesus' Name, Amen.

FAITH STATEMENT

MELANCHOLY NIGHT MEETS MORNING GLORY

"COLOR HER STORY"
FAVORED

"For Thou, Lord, wilt bless the righteous; with favor wilt Thou compass him as with a shield." Psalm 5:12 (KJV)

Favored: Feeling favored is like being the star of God's show, where your unique talents are celebrated and everything seems to align just right. Opportunities appear like exciting new paths just when you need them, and you keep riding the wave of God's favor. It's as if a strong wind is always at your back, guiding and supporting you, helping you shine and making your journey Angelic, supported every step of the way.

PRAYER FOR THE FAVORED

God, thank You for the blessing of favor in my life. Guide me with Your gentle winds, aligning my path with opportunities that allow my unique gifts to shine. I trust in Your support and divine connections at every step of my journey. In Jesus' Name, Amen.

FAITH STATEMENT

FAVOR IS GRACE REVEALING ITSELF

"COLOR HER STORY"

TIMID

"Be strong and of a good courage, fear not, nor be afraid of them: for the Lord thy God, he it is that doth go with thee; he will not fail thee, nor forsake thee." Deuteronomy 31:6 (KJV)

Timid. Imagine this: You begin as a "timid" woman, feeling shy and unsure of your place in the world. But, deep down, a spark ignites, fueled by a fierce determination to break free from the chains of self-doubt. You envision a future where you command rooms, confidently express your ideas, and shine with undeniable inner strength. You finally find your rightful place, feeling liberated because you're now free.

PRAYER FOR THE TIMID

God, I've been held back by fear and hesitation. I want to break free from worrying about other people's opinions of me and my negative self-image of myself. I need Your help to release fear and embrace Your love and walk in the confidence based on Your purpose for my life. In Jesus' Name, Amen.

FAITH STATEMENT

FAITH IS BUILT ONE STEP AT A TIME

"COLOR HER STORY"

HEALING

"Praise the Lord, my soul, and forget not all his benefits, who forgives all your sins and heals all your diseases." Psalm 103:2-3 (NIV)

Healing: In the gentle process of healing, you find renewal and strength, slowly mending the tender parts of your soul. This journey isn't a race but a personal evolution, where each day brings more solutions. As the scars of yesterday fade, they leave behind resilience and a deeper understanding from who you were made.

PRAYER FOR HEALING

God, I need Your help to heal the wounds in my emotions, body, mind, and relationships. Restore me to wholeness. Healing is one of Your greatest provisions for your children, and by your strips I am healed. In Jesus' Name, Amen.

FAITH STATEMENT

HEALING FOLLOWS LETTNG GO

"COLOR HER STORY"

UNBREAKABLE

"He only is my rock and my salvation: he is my defence; I shall not be moved." Psalm 62:6 (KJV)

Unbreakable: You are truly unbreakable, like a diamond formed under pressure. Everyone sees the beauty but not the sacrifices behind it. Only God knows the challenges you've overcome. Each trial and harsh word reveals your invincible spirit. Every tear and step you make only reinforce the fact that, with God, you bounce back every time. You are unbreakable because **God Is Real**.

PRAYER FOR BROKEN

Where do the strong go when they're weak? I am often called strong, I thank You, God, for the strength You've given me. Yet, even the strongest need help at times. Your words remind me I'm not alone; it's Your presence that truly makes me strong. In Jesus' Name, Amen.

FAITH STATEMENT

MY HELP COMES FROM GOD

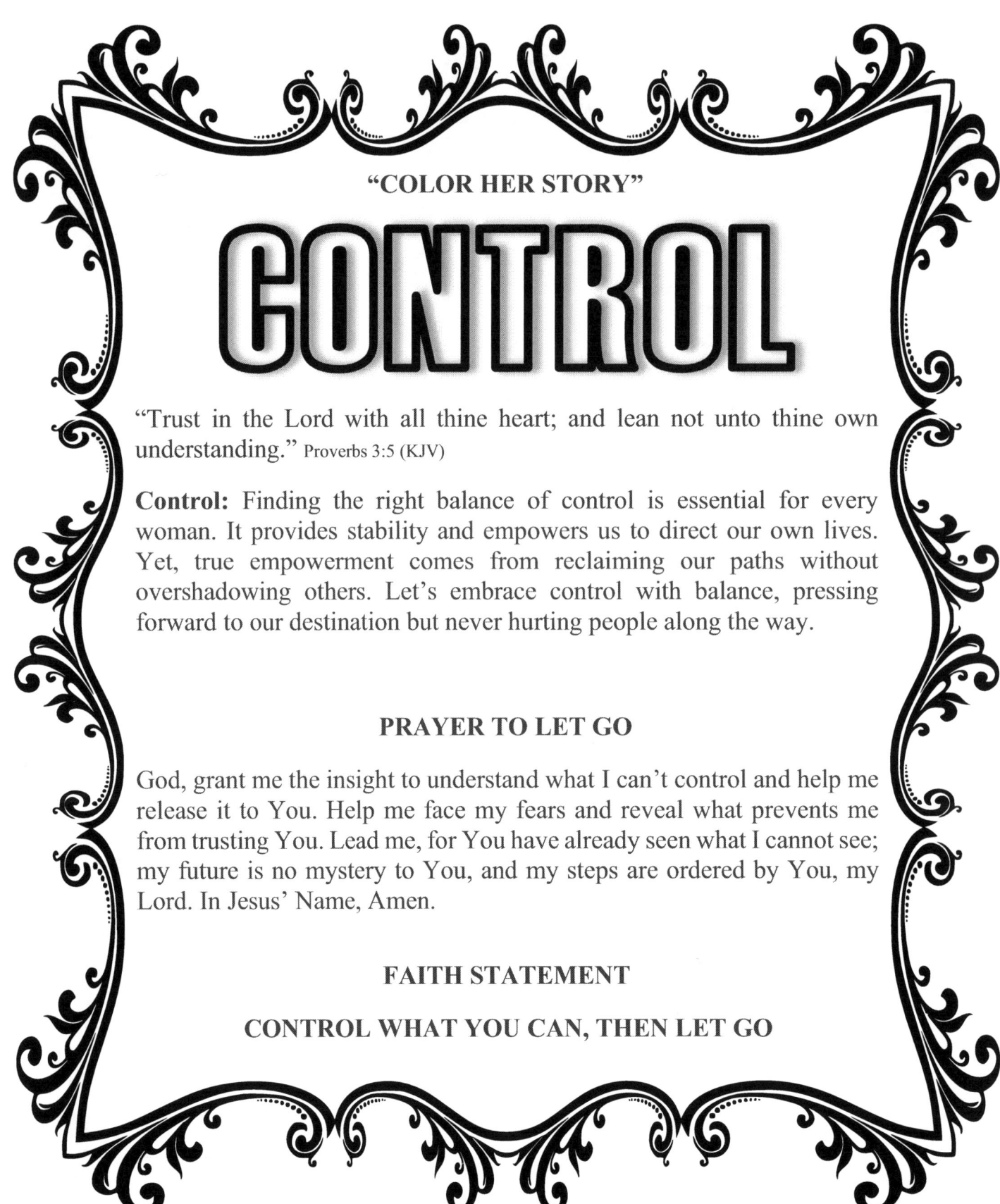

"COLOR HER STORY"

CONTROL

"Trust in the Lord with all thine heart; and lean not unto thine own understanding." Proverbs 3:5 (KJV)

Control: Finding the right balance of control is essential for every woman. It provides stability and empowers us to direct our own lives. Yet, true empowerment comes from reclaiming our paths without overshadowing others. Let's embrace control with balance, pressing forward to our destination but never hurting people along the way.

PRAYER TO LET GO

God, grant me the insight to understand what I can't control and help me release it to You. Help me face my fears and reveal what prevents me from trusting You. Lead me, for You have already seen what I cannot see; my future is no mystery to You, and my steps are ordered by You, my Lord. In Jesus' Name, Amen.

FAITH STATEMENT

CONTROL WHAT YOU CAN, THEN LET GO

"COLOR HER STORY"

CREATIVE

"For we are his workmanship, created in Christ Jesus unto good works, which God hath before ordained that we should walk in them."
Ephesians 2:10 (KJV)

Creative: Creativity is the ability to think outside the box and find solutions in everyday life that others find extremely hard. It's about using your unique insight to solve problems and express yourself. A creative person works smarter, not harder.

PRAYER FOR CREATIVITY

Dear God, I long to rekindle the dreamer within me. Life's challenges have dimmed my creative spirit, but I believe in Your power to reignite it with vibrant passion. Restore in me the joy of my salvation. In Jesus' Name, Amen.

FAITH STATEMENT

THE CREATIVE MIND IS ENDLESS

"COLOR HER STORY"
BETRAYED

"When my father and my mother forsake me, then the Lord will take me up." Psalm 27:10 (KJV)

Betrayed: Experiencing betrayal can be profoundly disheartening, especially in important relationships. However, these challenges can also provide clarity and direction. Though the initial hurt is intense, reflection often reveals deeper truths and lessons that guide future decisions. Embrace the insight gained, and let it help you move forward with greater understanding of relationships and how to choose them.

PRAYER FOR BETRAYAL

Betrayal is painful, and my heart hurts deeply. I really trusted, and I'm unsure if I can love again. Yet, I know only You, God, can heal my heart, I gave it to others; now I'm giving my heart to You. Even now—*WOW!*—I feel Your love and comfort, and I'm excited about living again to see everything You have planned for me. In Jesus' Name, Amen.

FAITH STATEMENT

BETRAYAL MAKES YOUR CHOICES CLEAR

"COLOR HER STORY"

ANTICIPATION

"For I know the plans I have for you, declares the Lord, plans for welfare and not for evil, to give you a future and a hope." Jeremiah 29:11 (ESV)

Anticipation: On the eve of New Year's, Lisa sat quietly by her window, gazing at the city lights and thinking about what the new year might bring. Full of anticipation, she made a list of dreams and goals she hoped to achieve, her heart racing with excitement at the fresh possibilities. What is your anticipation for tomorrow, next week, and next year? It begins with what you see today.

PRAYER FOR ANTICIPATION

Dear God, As I stand on the brink of not knowing what lies ahead, fill my heart with peace and patience. Grant me clarity and courage as I wait, and keep me free from anxiety and fear. Guide my steps and help me understand Your timing and plan for my life. In Jesus' Name, Amen.

FAITH STATEMENT

PATIENCE MEANS SURRENDERING TODAY

"COLOR HER STORY"

ADAPTABLE

"I know both how to be abased, and I know how to abound: everywhere and in all things, I am instructed both to be full and to be hungry, both to abound and to suffer need." Philippians 4:12 (KJV)

Adaptable: After losing her job unexpectedly, Celeste faced an uncertain future. Rather than despair, she prayed, sought wise counsel, and embraced the opportunity to learn new skills. Within months, Celeste transitioned into an entirely new career, showcasing her resilient and adaptable nature; she surprised herself.

PRAYER FOR BEING ADAPTABLE

God, adapting is challenging, as it involves facing the future, forgetting the past, and letting go of the present. Please help me confront the unknown and find balance in adapting to new things. I ask for wisdom to overcome all hidden fears. In Jesus' Name, Amen.

FAITH STATEMENT

NEW ENVIRONMENTS REQUIRE THAT WE ADAPT

"COLOR HER STORY"

BLESSED

"Blessed is the man that walketh not in the counsel of the ungodly, nor standeth in the way of sinners, nor sitteth in the seat of the scornful."
Psalm 1:1 (KJV)

Blessed: Being blessed is a state of obedience. It encompasses more than material and financial abundance, though these are definitely included. Many have wealth but aren't truly blessed. True blessing comes from fulfilling your God-given purpose and achieving your dreams. I am blessed because of Who blesses me.

PRAYER FOR BLESSED

God, I pray for forgiveness if I've been focused only on what I have rather than what You've done. Help me see my heart and honor You for who You are and how You've blessed me. In Jesus' Name, Amen.

FAITH STATEMENT

LET FAITH WRITE YOUR STORY

"COLOR HER STORY"

AMBITIOUS

"See thou a man diligent in his business? He shall stand before kings; he shall not stand before mean men." Proverbs 22:29 (KJV)

Ambition is like a fuel that drives me toward my dreams and encourages continual growth. It provides courage and opens up opportunities I might never have considered. However, it's essential to balance ambition to avoid stress and ensure it doesn't jeopardize my relationships and values. I strive to follow God's will and purpose for my life, prioritizing God's will over my own desires, considering my needs over the demands of people, and I must value people over material things.

PRAYER FOR THE AMBITIOUS

Dear Lord, Thank You for the ambition You've placed in me. Help me to use it wisely in line with Your will. Guide me to balance my dreams with love for others and faithfulness to You. May I always prioritize people over possessions and Your plans over my own desires. In Jesus' Name, Amen.

FAITH STATEMENT

SUCCESS IS DEFINED BY YOU

"COLOR HER STORY"

CLASSY

"She is clothed with strength and dignity; she can laugh at the days to come." Proverbs 31:25 (NIV)

Classy: Always poised and elegant, she has not just a touch of class but is classy in everything she does. A classy woman does not follow the trends in clothing or hair styles that others decide. Whether hosting a dinner party or presenting in a boardroom, she displays grace and sophistication that leaves an impression on everyone. She demands respect not with control but with her very presence' she is a classy lady.

PRAYER FOR THE CLASSY WOMAN

God, many don't understand. When we, as women, have to set a standard, we are often mislabeled for it. Give me the insight to deal with those who misunderstand who I am and who I desire to be. I need Your help when I am not accepted. In Jesus' Name, Amen.

FAITH STATEMENT

CLASS COMES FROM WITHIN; IT CANNOT BE BOUGHT

"COLOR HER STORY"

LOYAL

"A friend loveth at all times, and a brother is born for adversity."
Proverbs 17:17 (KJV)

Loyal: Debra's friendship was a treasure many sought. Her loyalty knew no bounds, as she consistently stood by her loved ones through thick and thin. During times of challenge and distress, I never had to reach out; she always sensed when I needed her and would appear by my side. I dedicate this to my loyal sister and friend, Debra, who is with the Lord but will always be in my heart.

PRAYER FOR THE LOYAL

Dear God, we ask for a heart of unwavering loyalty, to You, to our loved ones, and to the truth. Teach us to be steadfast and true, to be a source of trust and support for those around us. Help us to be loyal friends and partners, always carrying out our commitments with integrity and love. Guide us to act with kindness and honor in all our relationships, and give us the strength to stand by those we care for in times of need. In Jesus' Name, Amen.

FAITH STATEMENT

LOYALTY IS BIRTH FROM CHARACTER

"COLOR HER STORY"

HIDDEN

"For thou art my rock and my fortress; therefore, for thy name's sake, lead me and guide me. Pull me out of the net that they have laid privily for me, for thou art my strength." Psalm 31:3-4 (KJV)

Hidden: What secrets lie deep within your heart, holding you back with their hidden paths to the past? Embrace the challenge of releasing old pains and wounds while protecting the secret vows that secure your loyalty. Unlock the exciting potential of your future by transforming these burdens into stepping stones for your destiny.

PRAYER FOR HIDDEN BURDENS

God, heal burdens that are deep in my soul. Help me understand how to overcome what I have held as my private thoughts that bring pain and separation from those I love. I no longer want the guilt and torment of the hidden pain. In Jesus' Name, Amen.

FAITH STATEMENT

DIAMONDS ARE DISCOVERED IN HIDDEN PLACES

"COLOR HER STORY"

CONFIDENCE

"And this is the confidence that we have in him, that, if we ask any thing according to his will, he heareth us: And if we know that he hear us, whatsoever we ask, we know that we have the petitions that we desired of him." 1 John 5:14-15 (KJV)

Confidence: A confident woman feels sure of herself and is ready to take on challenges. However, if not balanced, confidence can become arrogance, leading her to dismiss others. A truly confident woman knows who she is, while recognizing the strength of others. Her confidence is not dependent on her feelings; it comes from an internal mirror that reflects who she truly is.

PRAYER FOR CONFIDENCE

God, help me during times I am searching for confidence. I want to trust You in every area of my life. I know You hear me when I pray; I trust that You will answer me, as you always do. In Jesus' Name, Amen.

FAITH STATEMENT

CONFIDENCE IS HOW I SEE MYSELF

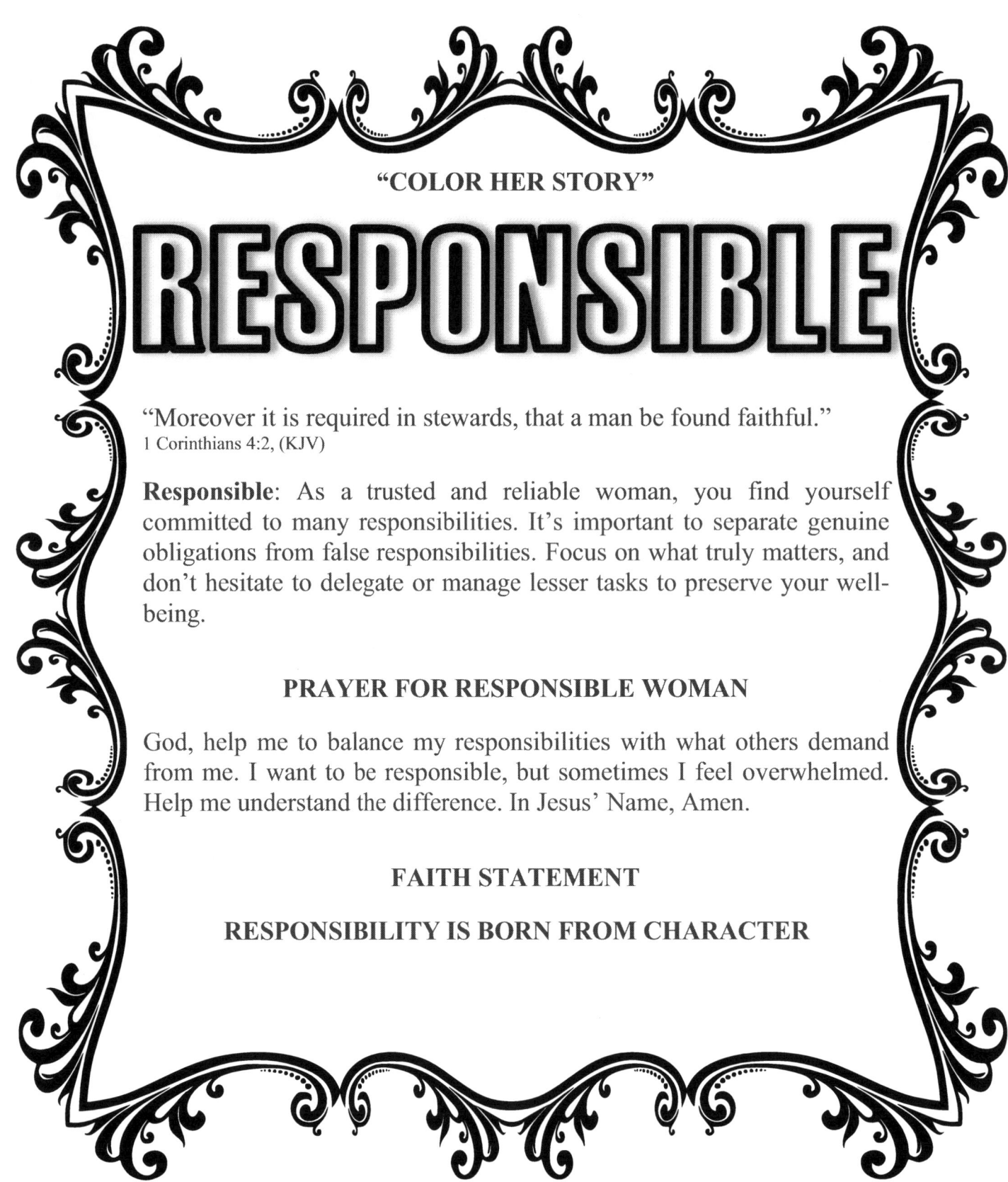

"COLOR HER STORY"
RESPONSIBLE

"Moreover it is required in stewards, that a man be found faithful."
1 Corinthians 4:2, (KJV)

Responsible: As a trusted and reliable woman, you find yourself committed to many responsibilities. It's important to separate genuine obligations from false responsibilities. Focus on what truly matters, and don't hesitate to delegate or manage lesser tasks to preserve your well-being.

PRAYER FOR RESPONSIBLE WOMAN

God, help me to balance my responsibilities with what others demand from me. I want to be responsible, but sometimes I feel overwhelmed. Help me understand the difference. In Jesus' Name, Amen.

FAITH STATEMENT

RESPONSIBILITY IS BORN FROM CHARACTER

"COLOR HER STORY"

DETERMINED

"I press toward the mark for the prize of the high calling of God in Christ Jesus." Philippians 3:14, (KJV)

Determined: A determined woman finishes what she starts. Her unwavering resolve sets her apart. Others admire her strength, yet few understand her relentless drive. She refuses to stop, proudly embracing her unique path and taking determined strides.

PRAYER FOR THE DETERMINED WOMAN

God, I pray for this determined woman. Grant her the strength and courage to pursue her dreams with wisdom. May she overcome challenges with grace, find balance, and accept support when needed. Remind her that seeking encouragement does not diminish her strength. In Jesus' Name, Amen.

FAITH STATEMENT

I WILL NEVER STOP

"COLOR HER STORY"

OPTIMISTIC

"For I know the thoughts that I think toward you, saith the Lord, thoughts of peace, and not of evil, to give you an expected end." Jeremiah 29:11 (KJV)

Optimistic: An optimistic woman sees hope and positivity where others see failure. She always finds a way to view things through a positive lens, inspiring those around her. Her outlook boosts spirits and sparks possibilities, yet she should remain mindful of potential risks and avoid being overly trusting. Embrace your optimism, but keep your eyes open, and you'll inspire change wherever you go!

PRAYER FOR THE OPTIMISTIC WOMAN

I want to be trusting and always see the good side of people, but I don't want to be foolish and unaware of those that are manipulative. God, give me the wisdom to know the difference. In Jesus' Name, Amen.

FAITH STATEMENT

SILVER LININGS ARE CLOSER THAN YOU THINK.

"COLOR HER STORY"

ORGANIZED

"Let all things be done decently and in order." 1 Corinthians 14:40 (KJV)

Organized: An organized woman keeps life running smoothly, whether at home or work, and strengthens family and friendships. However, being too rigid can hinder creativity. Use your skills effectively, but stay open and flexible to new ideas.

PRAYER FOR THE ORGANIZED WOMAN

God, help me, the organized woman. I need to find harmony between organizing and controlling my environment. Help me stay structured yet open to creativity. I don't want to be so focused on organizing that I forget to build the relationships around me. In Jesus' Name, Amen.

FAITH STATEMENT

**ORDER CLEARS THE PATH TO UNDERSTANDING"

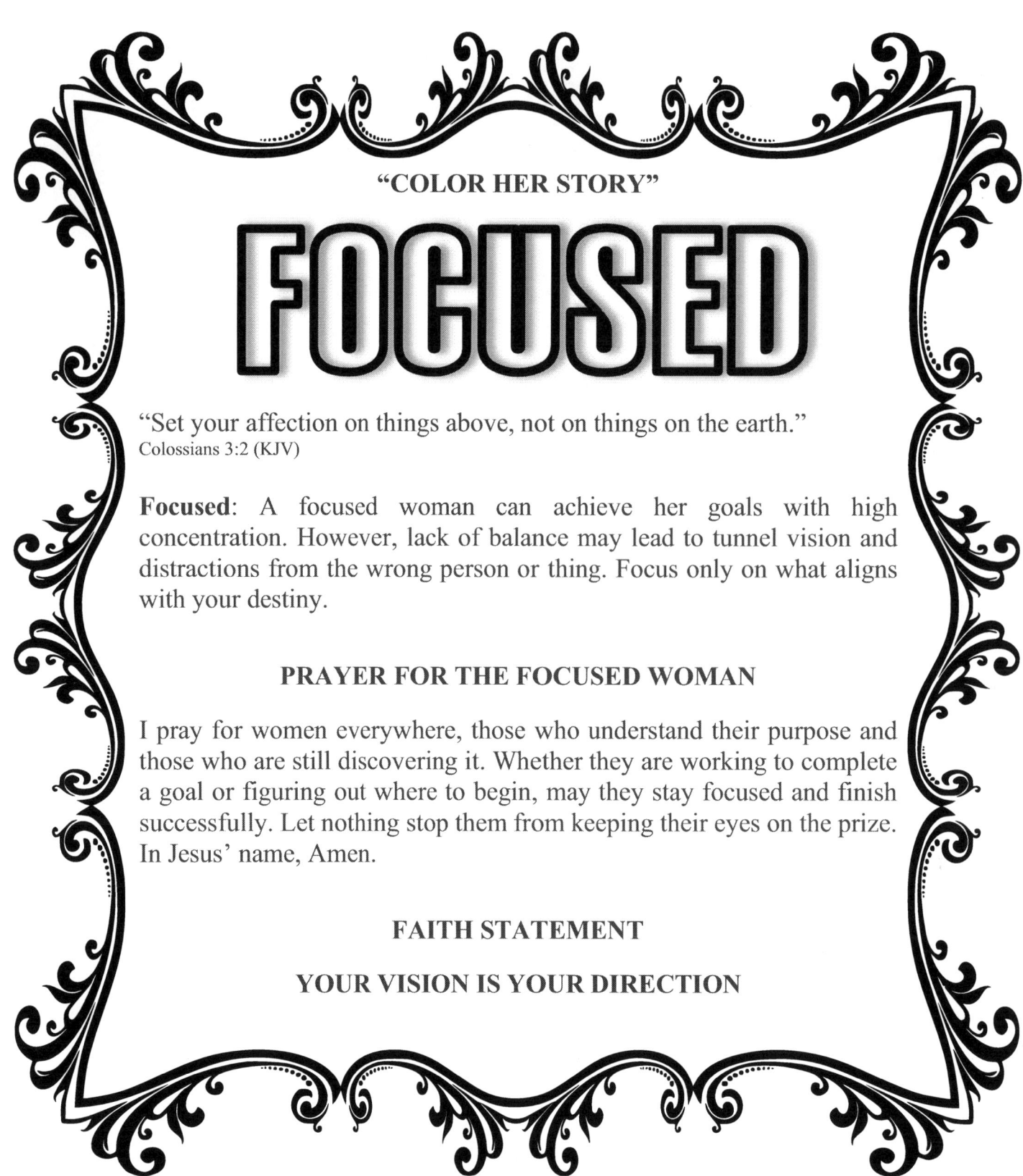

"COLOR HER STORY"

FOCUSED

"Set your affection on things above, not on things on the earth."
Colossians 3:2 (KJV)

Focused: A focused woman can achieve her goals with high concentration. However, lack of balance may lead to tunnel vision and distractions from the wrong person or thing. Focus only on what aligns with your destiny.

PRAYER FOR THE FOCUSED WOMAN

I pray for women everywhere, those who understand their purpose and those who are still discovering it. Whether they are working to complete a goal or figuring out where to begin, may they stay focused and finish successfully. Let nothing stop them from keeping their eyes on the prize. In Jesus' name, Amen.

FAITH STATEMENT

YOUR VISION IS YOUR DIRECTION

"COLOR HER STORY"
SURVIVOR

"I shall not die, but live, and declare the works of the Lord."
Psalm 118:17 (KJV)

Survivor: The woman survivor is resilient and has the ability to endure and overcome difficulties. She has survived many battles and very hard trials. The balance for her is not to develop a defensive or overly cautious mindset; this would affect her openness to new experiences.

PRAYER FOR WOMAN SURVIVOR

God, I need the strength, inner resilience, and courage in my heart, to embrace new experiences with trust and faith that I will survive every trial. In Jesus' Name, Amen.

FAITH STATEMENT

SECURE TOMORROW WITH YOUR THOUGHTS TODAY

"COLOR HER STORY"

REJECTION

"If the world hates you, keep in mind that it hated me first." John 15:18 (NIV)

Rejection often arises from insecurities or fears of abandonment, influencing how you interpret others' actions. It might also result from misunderstandings, jealousy, others' internal issues, or misaligned purposes.

Recognizing that rejection isn't always a refusal can be encouraging. It may indicate a need for personal change or a new direction. Use rejection as guidance. If the problem relates to your communication or behavior, make adjustments. However, if you're where you should be, don't let rejection deceive you to move from your true purpose. Instead, regroup and let transformation emerge from rejection.

PRAYER FOR REJECTION

In times of rejection, grant me the strength to see beyond the pain and recognize Your guidance toward better paths. Help me embrace redirection as growth, knowing that my worth is rooted in who You have chosen me to be, and not limited to how others see me. In Jesus' Name, Amen.

FAITH STATEMENT

REJECTION IS DIRECTION

"COLOR HER STORY"

INFERIOR

"And he said unto me, My grace is sufficient for thee: for my strength is made perfect in weakness. Most gladly therefore will I rather glory in my infirmities, that the power of Christ may rest upon me."
2 Corinthians 12:9 (KJV)

Inferior: A wise woman acknowledges areas for improvement but does not let feelings of inferiority lead to low self-esteem or prevent her from pursuing opportunities due to fear of inadequacy.

PRAYER FOR THE INFERIOR

God, when I feel insecure, help me understand that my strength comes from You. I exchange my weakness for Your strength. In Jesus' Name, Amen.

FAITH STATEMENT

EMBRACE WHO YOU ARE; REJECT INFERIOR THOUGHTS

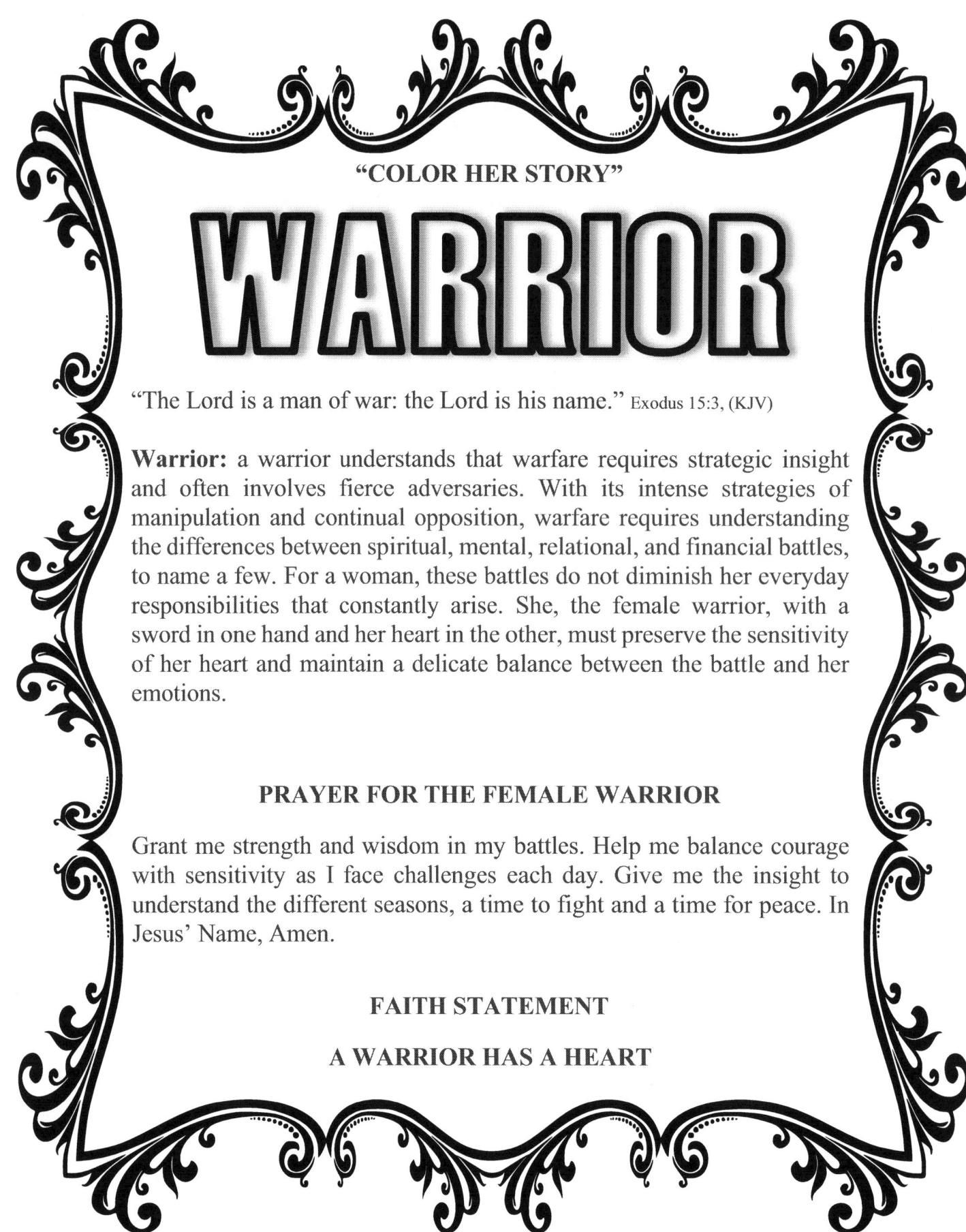

"COLOR HER STORY"
WARRIOR

"The Lord is a man of war: the Lord is his name." Exodus 15:3, (KJV)

Warrior: a warrior understands that warfare requires strategic insight and often involves fierce adversaries. With its intense strategies of manipulation and continual opposition, warfare requires understanding the differences between spiritual, mental, relational, and financial battles, to name a few. For a woman, these battles do not diminish her everyday responsibilities that constantly arise. She, the female warrior, with a sword in one hand and her heart in the other, must preserve the sensitivity of her heart and maintain a delicate balance between the battle and her emotions.

PRAYER FOR THE FEMALE WARRIOR

Grant me strength and wisdom in my battles. Help me balance courage with sensitivity as I face challenges each day. Give me the insight to understand the different seasons, a time to fight and a time for peace. In Jesus' Name, Amen.

FAITH STATEMENT

A WARRIOR HAS A HEART

"COLOR HER STORY"

IMMATURE

"Brethren, be not children in understanding: howbeit in malice be ye children, but in understanding be men." 1 Corinthians 14:20 (KJV)

Immature: An immature woman lacks experience and foresight, which can lead to her making impulsive decisions. There comes a time in every woman's life when she must make a decision to put away childish things and embrace the woman to be.

PRAYER FOR IMMATURITY

Grant me the wisdom to grow in maturity. Help me let go of childish ways and embrace patience, understanding, and responsibility. Guide me to reflect kindness and compassion. In Jesus' Name, Amen.

FAITH STATEMENT

MATURITY PUTS AWAY CHILDISH THINGS

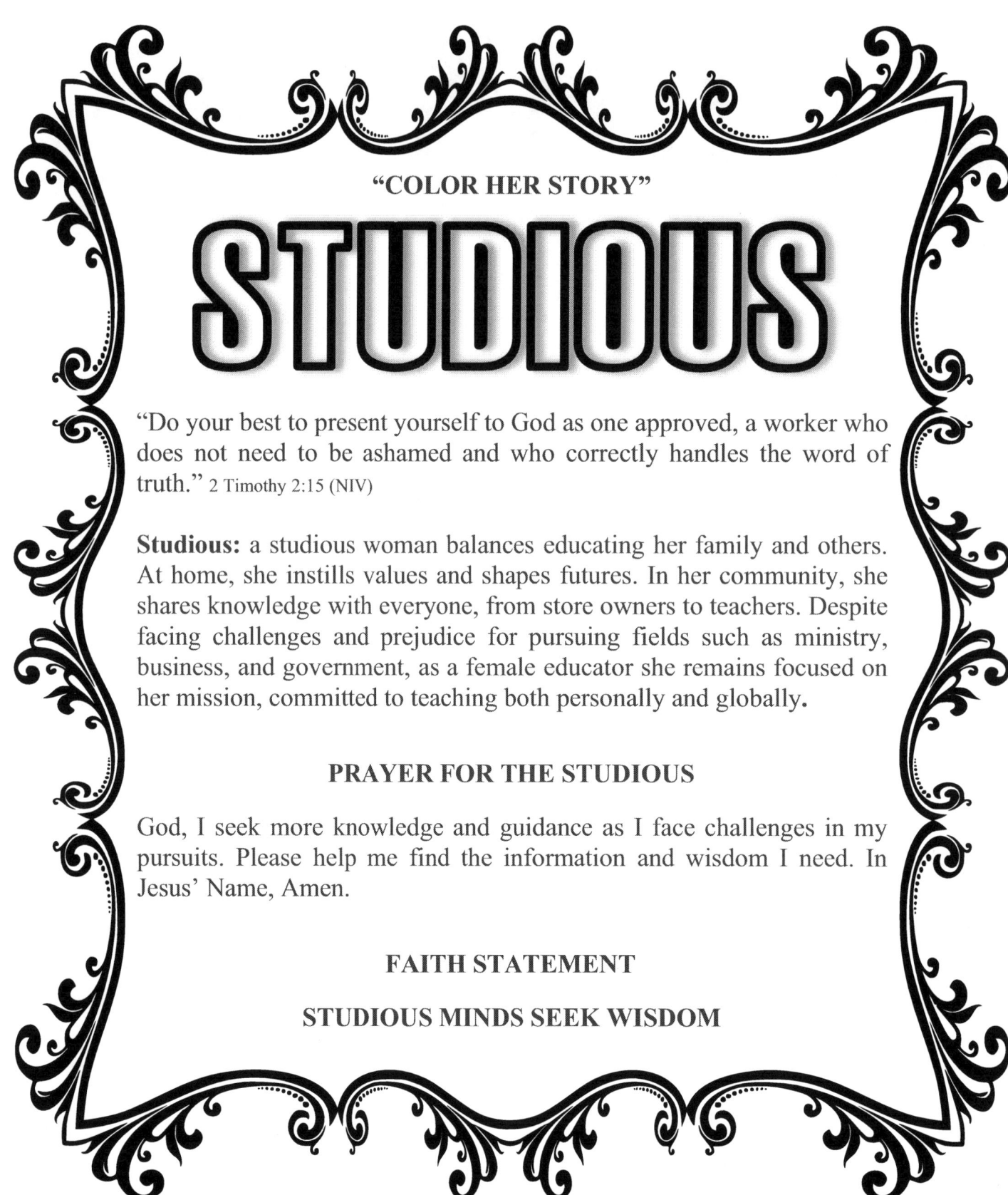

"COLOR HER STORY"

STUDIOUS

"Do your best to present yourself to God as one approved, a worker who does not need to be ashamed and who correctly handles the word of truth." 2 Timothy 2:15 (NIV)

Studious: a studious woman balances educating her family and others. At home, she instills values and shapes futures. In her community, she shares knowledge with everyone, from store owners to teachers. Despite facing challenges and prejudice for pursuing fields such as ministry, business, and government, as a female educator she remains focused on her mission, committed to teaching both personally and globally.

PRAYER FOR THE STUDIOUS

God, I seek more knowledge and guidance as I face challenges in my pursuits. Please help me find the information and wisdom I need. In Jesus' Name, Amen.

FAITH STATEMENT

STUDIOUS MINDS SEEK WISDOM

"COLOR HER STORY"

SHAME

"Anyone who believes in him will never be put to shame."
Romans 10:11 (NIV)

Shame: Shame can sting, but let it guide you, not define you. It's not a place to stay. Instead, let it spark growth and self-reflection after mistakes. Your choices shape your journey. Will it be one of shame or triumph? Choose the path to victory!

PRAYER FOR SHAME

God, help me with the shame from past mistakes and decisions. I need Your help to stop being so hard on myself. I hear You say to forgive myself, for You have forgiven me, and You are securing my future. In Jesus' Name, Amen.

FAITH STATEMENT

FORGIVENESS ERASES SHAME

"COLOR HER STORY"

GRACEFUL

"Let your conversation be always full of grace, seasoned with salt, so that you may know how to answer everyone." Colossians 4:6 (NIV)

Graceful: A graceful woman radiates elegance with ease; she is the very essence of femininity. Her remarkable presence requires careful balance so as not to seem untouchable or indifferent to the needs of others. With this balance, she inspires everyone around her.

PRAYER FOR THE GRACEFUL

I pray for Your grace and favor in areas I am pursuing. I trust You will go ahead of me as I face unknown paths; I will trust You. In Jesus' Name, Amen.

FAITH STATEMENT

GOD'S GRACE IS ENOUGH

"COLOR HER STORY"

TRIALS

"If thou faint in the day of adversity, thy strength is small." Proverbs 24:10 (KJV)

Trials: How we handle challenges is what truly matters, since trials reveal our true selves. Our behavior during difficult times indicates where we stood before the trial began. As the proverb says, "If you faint in the day of adversity, your strength is small." This suggests that how we respond to a trial can affect both its duration and the person we become afterward. Although trials are not easy, having a strategy to endure them is crucial. This approach will help us prevail against every storm, enabling us to emerge stronger.

PRAYER FOR OVERCOMING TRIALS

God, help me overcome fear in the midst of a trial. Give me insight for why I am here and what I need to do to move forward. A trial is a challenging thing, but with You I can do all things. In Jesus' Name, Amen.

FAITH STATEMENT

TRIALS TEST THE SUBSTANCE OF THE SOUL

"COLOR HER STORY"

AMAZED

"They were all amazed and glorified God, saying, 'We never saw anything like this!'" Mark 2:12 (NIV)

Amazed: At first, you're feeling discouraged, just going through the motions of daily life. But then, something unexpected happens, and everything starts turning in your favor. Suddenly, you're filled with amazement as doors that were once closed begin to swing open. You marvel at this transformation, knowing you couldn't have done it alone. Then, a still, small voice whispers to you, "Yes, it was Me, but, remember, you are amazing, too."

PRAYER THAT CREATES AMAZEMENT

God, I am so amazed by Your love and creativity. When I look at the sun and the stars, I see how magnificent You are. My prayer is to never forget to tell You how much I love You and to express my gratitude. Thank You. In Jesus' Name, Amen.

FAITH STATEMENT

GOD, THE WORKS OF YOUR HANDS ARE AMAZING

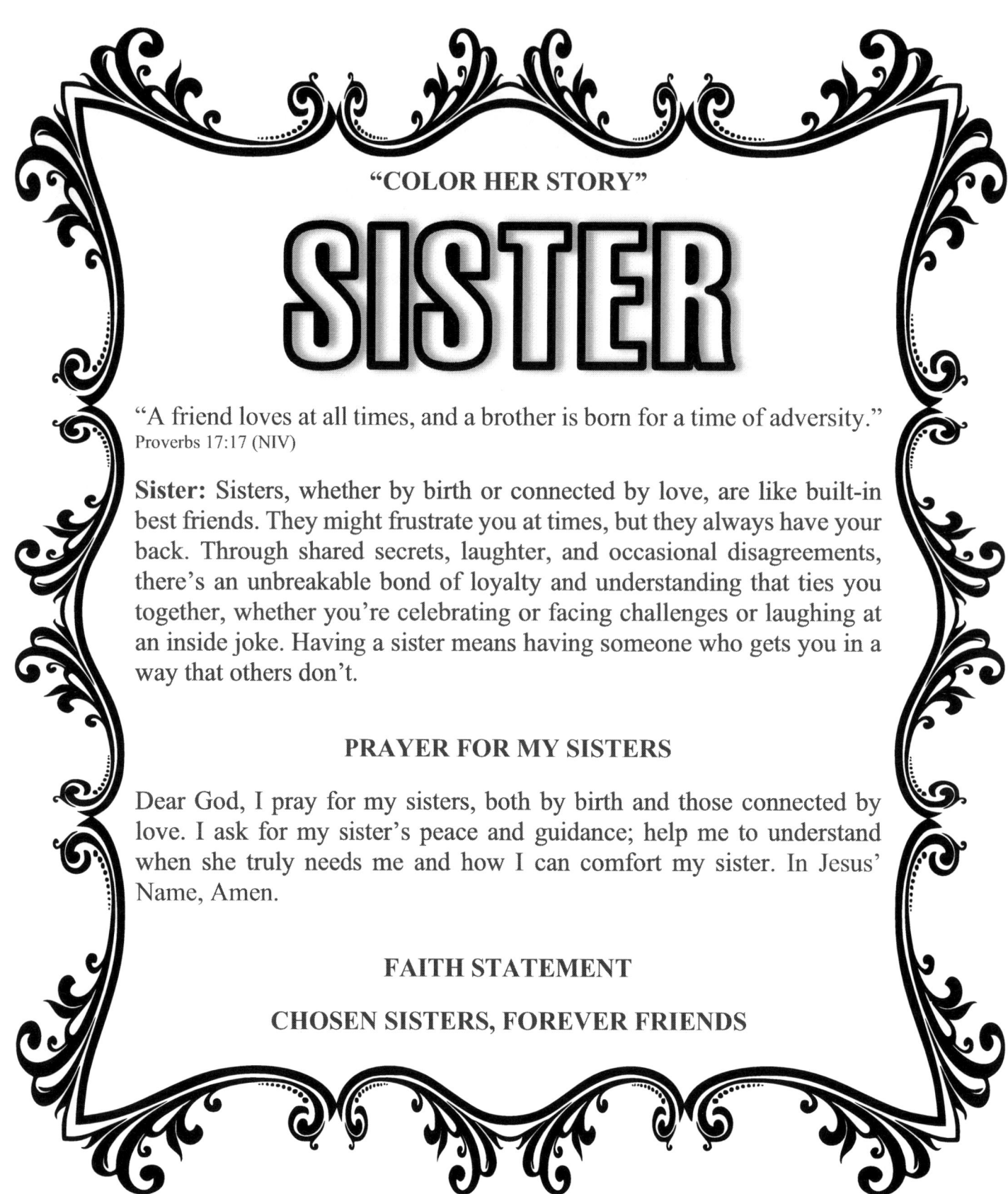

"COLOR HER STORY"

SISTER

"A friend loves at all times, and a brother is born for a time of adversity."
Proverbs 17:17 (NIV)

Sister: Sisters, whether by birth or connected by love, are like built-in best friends. They might frustrate you at times, but they always have your back. Through shared secrets, laughter, and occasional disagreements, there's an unbreakable bond of loyalty and understanding that ties you together, whether you're celebrating or facing challenges or laughing at an inside joke. Having a sister means having someone who gets you in a way that others don't.

PRAYER FOR MY SISTERS

Dear God, I pray for my sisters, both by birth and those connected by love. I ask for my sister's peace and guidance; help me to understand when she truly needs me and how I can comfort my sister. In Jesus' Name, Amen.

FAITH STATEMENT

CHOSEN SISTERS, FOREVER FRIENDS

"COLOR HER STORY"

FAITH

"Now faith is the substance of things hoped for, the evidence of things not seen." Hebrews 11:1 (KJV)

Faith is confidence in what we cannot see, the essential force that holds space for what must manifest. It becomes the substance, reserving the presence of what is to come. Faith brings fulfillment while we wait, overcoming fear by envisioning the future within the lens of faith. It serves as your evidence of the things you hope and long for; without faith, it is impossible to please God. For dreamers and visionaries, the main element is **FAITH**.

PRAYER FOR FAITH

God, help me find strength in my faith and the courage to face challenges with hope. Guide me to remain open-minded and balance my beliefs with wisdom and understanding. In Jesus' Name, Amen.

FAITH STATEMENT

FAITH HAS SUBSTANCE

"COLOR HER STORY"

JOY

"The joy of the Lord is your strength." Nehemiah 8:10 (NIV)

Joy: When a woman is blessed, the joy seen in her eyes is truly uplifting. Unlike happiness, which is a natural emotion, joy comes from God and is part of His nature. When a woman is filled with this divine joy, it radiates to her family, friends, and everyone she meets, for the joy of the Lord is her strength

PRAYER FOR JOY

Dear God, please fill me with Your joy and strength in times of trouble. Help me to see through Your eyes, beyond my circumstances. In Jesus' Name, Amen.

FAITH STATEMENT

THE JOY OF THE LORD IS MY STRENGTH

"COLOR HER STORY"

TROUBLE

"God is our refuge and strength, an ever-present help in trouble."
Psalm 46:1 (NIV)

Trouble can be tough, since it causes stress, disrupts our lives, and strains relationships. However, trouble also signals several things.

1. Trouble signifies someone or something has disrupted our lives
2. Trouble urges us to seek God's strength
3. Trouble is seasonal
4. Trouble can teach important lessons
5. Trouble helps us appreciate peaceful times
6. Trouble encourages problem-resolution
7. Trouble has an expiration date

PRAYER FOR TROUBLE

God, Your power surpasses all trouble. Help me see through Your eyes. You are my refuge in times of need. You've delivered me before, and I trust You'll deliver me again. In Jesus' Name, Amen.

FAITH STATEMENT

TROUBLE DEMANDS SOLUTIONS

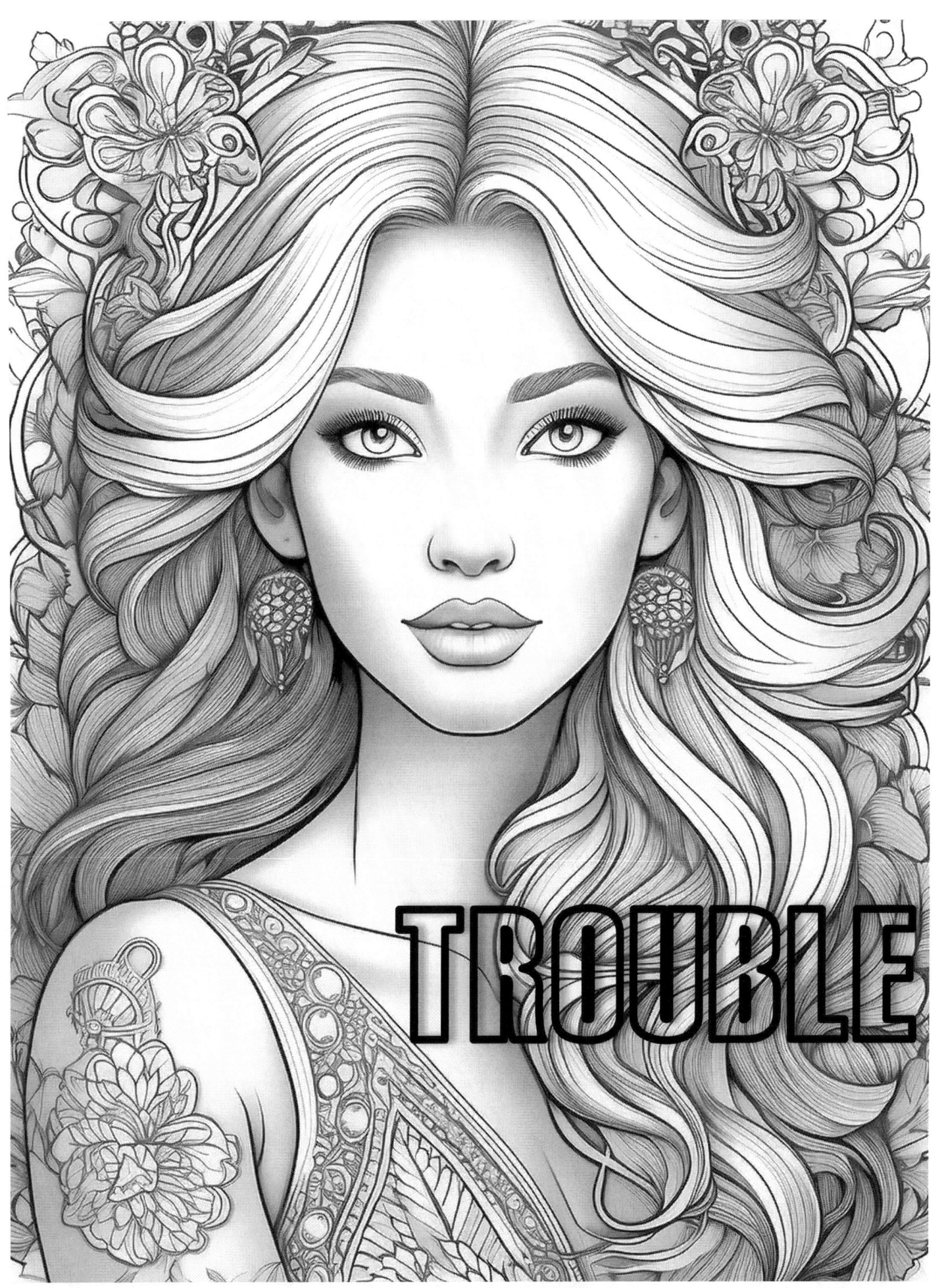

"COLOR HER STORY"
FUNNY

"A cheerful heart is good medicine, but a crushed spirit dries up the bones." Proverbs 17:22 (NIV)

Funny: A woman with humor brings joy and excitement. While laughing is fun, remember it's important to avoid humor that could be seen as insensitive or sarcastic. Enjoy making people smile, while never laughing at their expense.

PRAYER FOR THE WOMAN WHO DESIRES FUN

God, help me embrace a day filled with joy and laughter. I'm grateful for what I have and trust that You will provide what I need. Guide me to find fun and enjoyment while honoring wisdom, ensuring that my humor is never sarcastic in a way that harms others. Search my heart, Lord, so I may share laughter with the intent to encourage and uplift those around me. In Jesus' Name, Amen.

FAITH STATEMENT

LAUGH; IT'S CONTAGIOUS

"COLOR HER STORY"

PEACE

"Peace I leave with you; my peace I give you. I do not give to you as the world gives. Do not let your hearts be troubled, and do not be afraid."
John (14:27)

Peace is necessary to stabilize an environment; it is a force for building strong relationships. However, sometimes seeking peace might cause us to shy away from necessary confrontations, preventing us from dealing with important issues that need to be addressed. Peace should not be confused with passiveness. Avoidance of conflict can lead to unresolved tensions. True peace isn't just about avoiding conflicts; it's about creating a world where people understand and respect each other.

PRAYER FOR PEACE

God, I desire peace in every situation and relationship. When I am uncertain, give me peace. I desire to live a life with love and peace as the ruling forces of my life. In Jesus' Name, Amen.

FAITH STATEMENT

PEACE BEGINS WITHIN

"COLOR HER STORY"

DARING

"Be strong and courageous. Do not be afraid; do not be discouraged, for the Lord your God will be with you wherever you go." Joshua 1:9 (NIV)

Daring: A daring woman is guided by her purpose and desires. She is innovative, challenges norms, and pushes boundaries. However, she must maintain a balance by exercising wisdom to ensure she doesn't take uncalulated risks that could jeopardize her safety and peace of mind.

PRAYER FOR THE DARING

Lord, grant me balance and humility. Help me to embrace peace and avoid competition, and remind me to stay grounded when I feel in control. In Jesus' Name, Amen.

FAITH STATEMENT

I DARE TO BE DIFFERENT

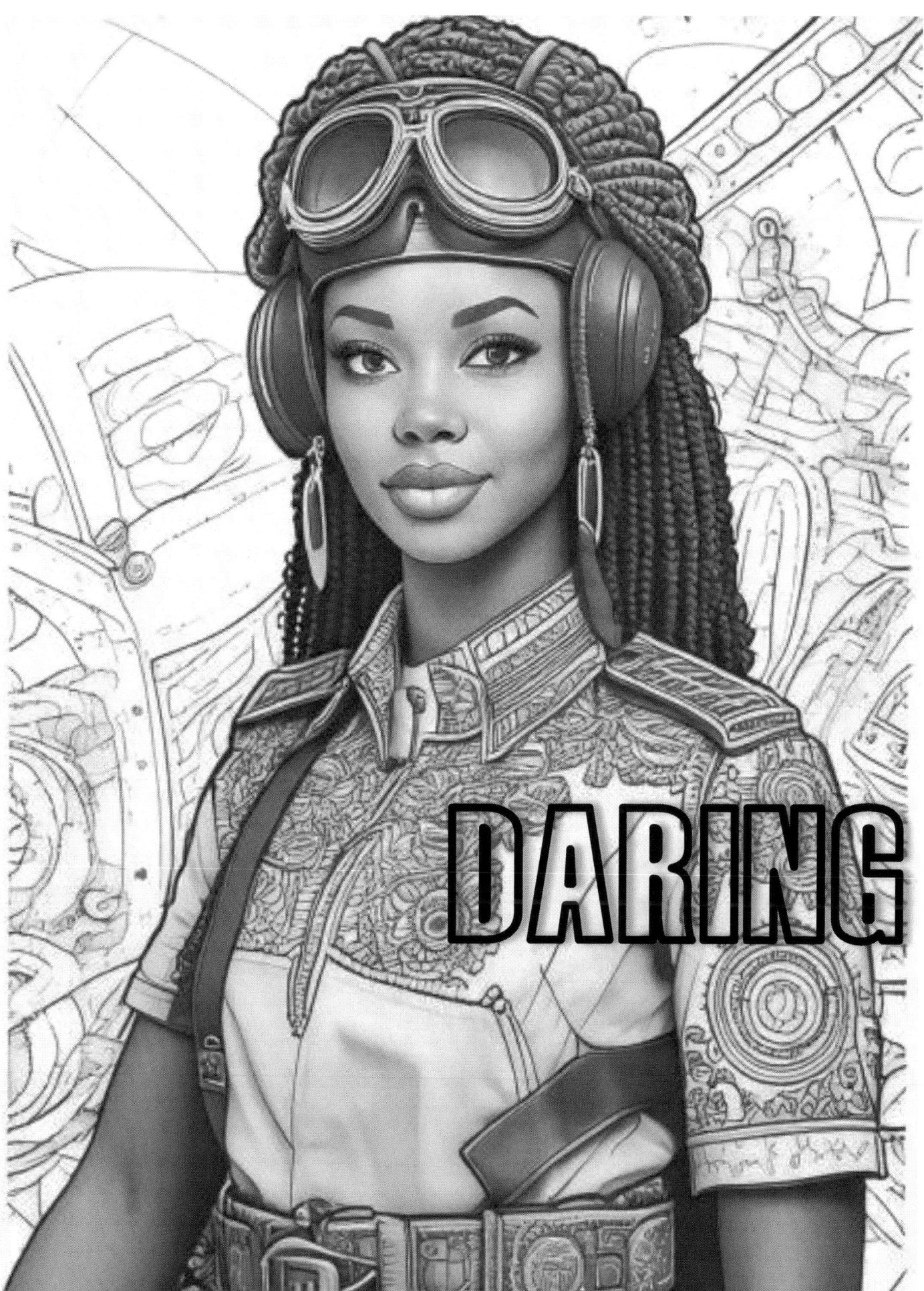

"COLOR HER STORY"

REST

"Come to me, all you who are weary and burdened, and I will give you rest." Matthew 11:28 (NIV)

Rest: Embracing rest and recovery is essential for everyone, especially for women. Taking time to rest helps restore both your physical and mental well-being. One of the biggest challenges is to take care of yourself while caring for others.

PRAYER FOR REST

Lord, give me peace and calm. I need rest. Heal my mind and body, and shield me with Your protection. Bless me to awake refreshed and renewed, ready and recovered for the days ahead. In Jesus' Name, Amen.

FAITH STATEMENT

REST AND RECOVER

"COLOR HER STORY"

FEARLESS

"For God hath not given us the spirit of fear; but of power, and of love, and of a sound mind." 2 Timothy 1:7 (KJV)

Fearless: A fearless woman may sometimes be misunderstood as someone who is heartless, but this couldn't be further from the truth. Her bravery does not negate her capacity for compassion and empathy. The balance for a fearless woman lies in being courageous while also embracing and honoring her sensitivity.

PRAYER FOR THE FEARLESS

God, You are the only place the fearless can come and get strength in times of trouble I pray You restore me, for I truly know my help comes from You. In Jesus' Name, Amen.

FAITH STATEMENT

FEAR IS FALSE EVIDENCE APPEARING REAL

"COLOR HER STORY"

BALANCED

"The path of the righteous is level; you, the Upright One, make the way of the righteous smooth." Isaiah 26:7 (NIV)

Balanced: Women often juggle many roles, from family and friends to work and more. To find balance, it's crucial to know your own limits and responsibilities. Once you've identified these priorities, relax and make decisions about what's next.

PRAYER FOR BALANCE

God, give me balance in the midst of so many demands. I need Your help when I am surrounded by so many unfinished things. Help me remember that a lack of balance will hinder clear directions. In Jesus' Name, Amen.

FAITH STATEMENT

BALANCE DEMANDS DISCIPLINE

"COLOR HER STORY"

SECURE

"The Lord is my rock, my fortress and my deliverer; my God is my rock, in whom I take refuge." Psalm 18:2 (NIV)

Secure: Every woman needs to feel secure, as it brings safety and confidence. However, over-focusing on security can lead to fear and make it hard to embrace change. It's important to find a balance by first seeking security from God, which can help heal hidden fears and insecurities. Secondly, become confident that you are the one chosen to finish your course.

PRAYER FOR SECURITY

God, You are my rock. I will run to You in times of fear and insecurity. Give me peace in the midst of trouble. My trust is in You, my strong tower. In Jesus' Name, Amen.

FAITH STATEMENT

GOD IS MY STRONG TOWER

"COLOR HER STORY"
SILENT

"A time to tear and a time to mend, a time to be silent and a time to speak."
Ecclesiastes 3:7 (NIV)

Silent: Because a woman often loves to talk, her silence can speak volumes. It may mean she is hurt or reflecting. Sometimes her silence is not just a cry for help but the demands of her stubbornness. This woman may still need love and support, but not in the way she demands it. Every woman is unique and requires patience. To truly support a woman, learn to understand her laughter, tears, and fears, but, most importantly, recognize her silence.

PRAYER FOR THE SILENT

God, during the times I don't fully understand, help me identify my true feelings. Silence at the wrong time is not proper communication. I want to have balance between being silent and speaking at the right time. In Jesus' Name, Amen.

FAITH STATEMENT

SILENCE SPEAKS VOLUMES

"COLOR HER STORY"

ALONE

"Can two walk together, except they be agreed?" Amos 3:3 (KJV)

Alone: Walking alone can be challenging and isolating for a woman; family, friendships, and community are invaluable for sharing experiences. However, there are times when being alone is necessary to protect your physical and mental health. Loneliness can also be an opportunity to start a hobby or tap into your creativity. Prioritizing self-love over toxic relationships is not selfishness; it's called self-preservation.

PRAYER FOR THE WOMAN ALONE

Dear God, in times of solitude, I seek Your presence to fill my heart, turning loneliness into an opportunity for a deeper relationship with You. Please grant me the wisdom to form meaningful relationships that support my purpose, beyond just filling the void of loneliness. In Jesus' Name, Amen.

FAITH STATEMENT

ALONE, NOT LONELY

"COLOR HER STORY"

CRITICISM

"Listen to advice and accept discipline, and at the end you will be counted among the wise." Proverbs 19:20 (NIV)

Criticism can be a double-edged sword. On one hand, it's an expression of disapproval that feels very harsh and unfair, especially when it targets women for their appearance, clothing, or marital status. On the other hand, to criticize is to analyze, which can offer constructive examination, helping us improve. Often, the most damaging criticism is self-criticism, creating self-sabotage and a negative self-image. Always remember, there is only one you. Your fingerprint is proof that you were meant to be the unique and awesome YOU.

PRAYER FOR THE CRITICIZED

God, when I face criticism and judgment, help me to recognize any bitterness in my heart from persecution and those who judge me by my appearance or choices or simply because I love You. When it's my fault, I repent; when its persecution, I need insight and understanding how to model Your example, "to love them, for they know not what they do." In Jesus' Name, Amen.

FAITH STATEMENT

CRITICISM CAN SHARPEN OR DULL YOUR EDGE

"COLOR HER STORY"
BROKEN

"The Lord is close to the brokenhearted and saves those who are crushed in spirit." Psalm 34:18 (NIV)

Broken: Experiencing brokenness can be incredibly challenging for women, often leading to feelings of pain and self-doubt. However, it also presents opportunities for personal development and maturity. Facing these challenges head on can lead to newfound confidence and wisdom. It's like finding treasures after a storm: you understand yourself better and appreciate not the trial but what you learned through it.

PRAYER FOR THE BROKEN

God, when I face criticism and judgment, help me to recognize any bitterness in my heart from persecution and those who judge me by my appearance or choices or simply because I love You. When it's my fault, I repent; when its persecution, I need insight and understanding how to model Your example, "to love them, for they know not what they do." In Jesus' Name, Amen.

FAITH STATEMENT

BROKEN YET MATURING

"COLOR HER STORY"

RESERVED

"Even a fool is thought wise if he keeps silent, and discerning if he holds his tongue." Proverbs 17:28 (NIV)

Reserved: A person with a reserved nature is like someone who observes the world through a thoughtful lens before jumping in. A reserved nature is a practice in mindful decision-making. It adds depth to your presence. However, being too reserved might make it harder to bond deeply with others, leading some to misinterpret your intentions.

PRAYER FOR THE RESERVED

Dear God, I come before You seeking guidance and love, unsure of whom I can trust, yet open to Your embrace. Teach me to embrace my true self and step forward in relationships with confidence. Let Your wisdom guide me and Your love fill my heart. In Jesus' Name, Amen.

FAITH STATEMENT

THE QUIET HEART HOLDS GREAT WISDOM.

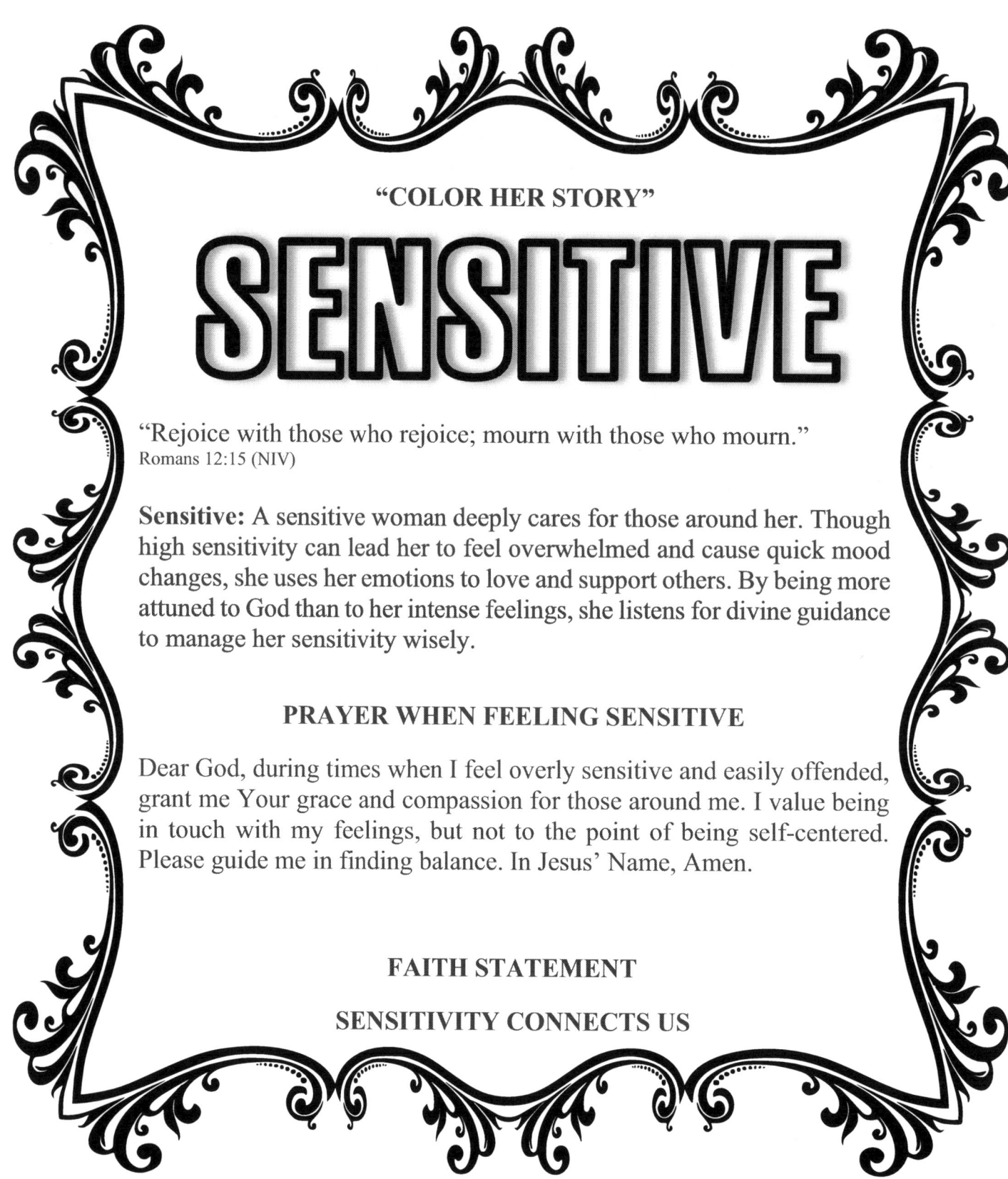

"COLOR HER STORY"

SENSITIVE

"Rejoice with those who rejoice; mourn with those who mourn."
Romans 12:15 (NIV)

Sensitive: A sensitive woman deeply cares for those around her. Though high sensitivity can lead her to feel overwhelmed and cause quick mood changes, she uses her emotions to love and support others. By being more attuned to God than to her intense feelings, she listens for divine guidance to manage her sensitivity wisely.

PRAYER WHEN FEELING SENSITIVE

Dear God, during times when I feel overly sensitive and easily offended, grant me Your grace and compassion for those around me. I value being in touch with my feelings, but not to the point of being self-centered. Please guide me in finding balance. In Jesus' Name, Amen.

FAITH STATEMENT

SENSITIVITY CONNECTS US

"COLOR HER STORY"

ASSURANCE

"Let us draw near with a true heart in full assurance of faith, having our hearts sprinkled from an evil conscience, and our bodies washed with pure water." Hebrews 10:22 (KJV)

Assurance: A woman with assurance possesses confidence and a sense of certainty, often rooted in faith and conviction. However, it's important for her to balance this assurance to avoid overconfidence, which can lead to self-righteousness and a lack of humility, preventing her from listening to others' truths.

PRAYER FOR ASSURANCE

Dear God, in a world full of uncertainties, I need the assurance that my future is secure. When I feel a lack of confidence, please give me the insight I need to find inner peace that only comes from You. In Jesus' Name, Amen.

FAITH STATEMENT

ASSURANCE IS THE QUIET WHISPER OF CERTAINTY

"COLOR HER STORY"
FINISHER

"Being confident of this, that he who began a good work in you will carry it on to completion until the day of Christ Jesus." Philippians 1:6 (NIV)

Finisher: A woman possessing the spirit of a finisher moves like the winds of a tornado. This force, given to her by way of her divine purpose and those she loves, is fueled by a deep-seated determination to see every task through to the end.

Energized by her vision, she charges forward with an electrifying blend of passion and perseverance. Though her eyes are fixed on the finish line, she knows that true fulfillment comes from being patient and embracing the journey itself—the lessons learned, the obstacles conquered, and the creativity guiding her steps along the way. She has the spirit of a **FINISHER.**

PRAYER FOR THE FINISHER

Lord, help me to finish what I've started. Only You know the future, so please guide me to live fully in today while envisioning tomorrow. I trust that tomorrow is secure because You have gone ahead of me and made the crooked places straight. In Jesus' Name, Amen.

FAITH STATEMENT

A FINISHER SEES THE END

HER STORIES—TABLE OF CONTENTS

About the Author 1

"COLOR HER STORY" Introduction 3

PURPOSE 4

PERSERVERANCE 6

DREAMER 8

VISIONARY 10

EMPOWERED 12

COMMITTED 14

SECRETS 16

REGRET 18

FRIEND 20

MOODS 22

WORRY 24

FEAR 26

ANGER 28

HURT 30

ABANDONED 32

REVENGE 34

WRONGED 36

FAITHFUL 38

TEACHER 40

CAUTIOUS 42

ASSERTIVE 44

WEEPING 46

STRATEGIC 48

BRAVE 50

HARDSHIP 52

BARRIERS 54

ISOLATION	56
PATIENCE	58
COURAGEOUS	60
CONCERNED	62
RESENTFUL	64
INSECURITY	66
DYNAMIC	68
SERENITY	70
THOUGHTFUL	72
DELILAH	74
EXPECTATION	76
TENACIOUS	78
FORGIVE	80
PAIN	82
DOUBT	84
CALM	86
SADNESS	88
BOLD	90
ANXIETY	92
LOVED	94
MATURE	96
RESILIENT	98
ARTIST	100
SHYNESS	102
MELANCHOLY	104
FAVORED	106
TIMID	108
HEALING	110
UNBREAKABLE	112
CONTROL	114
CREATIVE	116

BETRAYED	118
ANTICIPATION	120
ADAPTABLE	122
BLESSED	124
AMBITIOUS	126
CLASSY	128
LOYAL	130
HIDDEN	132
CONFIDENCE	134
RESPONSIBLE	136
DETERMINED	138
OPTIMISTIC	140
ORGANIZED	142
FOCUSED	144
SURVIVOR	146
REJECTION	148
INFERIOR	150
WARRIOR	152
IMMATURE	154
STUDIOUS	156
SHAME	158
GRACEFUL	160
TRIALS	162
AMAZED	164
SISTER	166
FAITH	168
JOY	170
TROUBLE	172
FUNNY	174
PEACE	176

DARING	178
REST	180
FEARLESS	182
BALANCED	184
SECURE	186
SILENT	188
ALONE	190
CRITICISM	192
BROKEN	194
RESERVED	196
SENSITIVE	198
ASSURANCE	200
FINISHER	202

HER STORIES—INDEX

ABANDONED	32
ADAPTABLE	122
ALONE	190
AMAZED	164
AMBITIOUS	126
ANGER	28
ANTICIPATION	120
ANXIETY	92
ARTIST	100
ASSERTIVE	44
ASSURANCE	200
BALANCED	184
BARRIERS	54
BETRAYED	118
BLESSED	124
BOLD	90
BRAVE	50
BROKEN	194
CALM	86
CAUTIOUS	42
CLASSY	128
COMMITTED	14
CONCERNED	62
CONFIDENCE	134
CONTROL	114
COURAGEOUS	60
CREATIVE	116
CRITICISM	192
DARING	178
DELILAH	74
DETERMINED	138
DOUBT	84
DREAMER	8
DYNAMIC	68
EMPOWERED	12
EXPECTATION	76
FAITH	168
FAITHFUL	38
FAVORED	106
FEAR	26

FEARLESS	182
FINISHER	202
FOCUSED	144
FORGIVE	80
FRIEND	20
FUNNY	174
GRACEFUL	160
HARDSHIP	52
HEALING	110
HIDDEN	132
HURT	30
IMMATURE	154
INFERIOR	150
INSECURITY	66
ISOLATION	56
JOY	170
LOVED	94
LOYAL	130
MATURE	96
MELANCHOLY	104
MOODS	22
OPTIMISTIC	140

ORGANIZED	142
PAIN	82
PATIENCE	58
PEACE	176
PERSERVERANCE	6
PURPOSE	4
REGRET	18
REJECTION	148
RESENTFUL	64
RESERVED	196
RESILIENT	98
RESPONSIBLE	136
REST	180
REVENGE	34
SADNESS	88
SECRETS	16
SECURE	186
SENSITIVE	198
SERENITY	70
SHAME	158
SHYNESS	102
SILENT	188

SISTER	166
STRATEGIC	48
STUDIOUS	156
SURVIVOR	146
TEACHER	40
TENACIOUS	78
THOUGHTFUL	72
TIMID	108
TRIALS	162
TROUBLE	172
UNBREAKABLE	112
VISIONARY	10
WARRIOR	152
WEEPING	46
WORRY	24
WRONGED	36

Made in the USA
Columbia, SC
27 May 2025